Bangkok in a Nutshell

A *real* pocket guide to Thailand's
City of Angels

ERIC ARCHER

Bangkok in a Nutshell

A *real* pocket guide to Thailand's
City of Angels

Asia Revealed Publishing Company

Copy Right Asia Revealed Publishing Company
All rights reserved. No textual part of this publication may be reproduced, stored in a retrieval system, or transmitted, in any form or by any means, without the prior permission in writing from the publisher, nor be otherwise circulated in any form of binding or cover other than that in which it is published without a similar condition of approval.

©2017 by Asia Revealed Publishing Company
Cover: Creative Commons CCO,
including for commercial purposes
Publisher: Asia Revealed Publishing Company,
Weston-super-Mare, United Kingdom
Print: Ingram/Lightning Source
ISBN: 978-1-912414-02-4

CONTENT

Preface 15

Arriving to Bangkok 17

    Taxi 18

    Airport Limousine 19

    Airport Rail Link 19

    Local Bus BMTA 20

    Public Van (minibus) 20

    Coach 21

Public Transportation in Bangkok 22

    Skytrain and Subway 22

    Skytrain 22

    Subway 24

    Express Boats on Chao Phraya River 24

    Canal Boats 25

    Ferry 26

- Buses 27
- Taxis, Tuk-Tuks, and Motorcycles 29
  - Taxis 29
  - Tuk-Tuks 30
  - Motorcycle Taxis 31
- Exploring Bangkok 32
  - Bangkok 33
- China Town 37
  - Tourist Destinations in China Town 38
  - Temples in China Town 39
  - Markets in China Town 39
- The River Chao Phraya 41
  - Koh Kret 41
  - River Cruises 43
  - Ayutthaya 44
- Parks in Bangkok 46
  - Benjasiri Park 47

- Lumpini Park 48
- Rot Fai Park 49
- Suan Luang Rama 9 Park 51

Shopping Malls 53
- MBK 54
- Downtown Siam 55
- The Emporium 57
- Terminal 21 58
- Asiatique: The River Front 59
- Pantip Plaza 60

Markets in Bangkok 62
- Chatuchak Weekend Market 62
- Pratunam Market 63
- Bo Bae Market 65

Floating Markets 66
- Damnoen Saduak Floating Market 66
- Amphawa Floating Market 67

    Taling Chan Floating Market 68

Night Markets 70

    Khaosan Road 70

    Patpong Night Market 71

    Rot Fai Market.. 72

    Suan Lum Night Bazaar Ratchada 73

A Bangkok for Children 75

    Art in Paradise 75

    Bounce 76

    Dinosaur Planet 77

    Dream World... 78

    Dusit Zoo 79

    KidZania 80

    Madame Tussauds 82

    Safari World 83

    Sea Life Bangkok Ocean World 84

    Suan Siam Water Park/Siam Park City 85

The Temples of Bangkok 87
Wat Arun: Temple of Dawn............................ 88
The Grand Palace and Wat Phra Kaew........... 89
Wat Pho: Temple of the Reclining Buddha 91

Unusual and Unique Restaurants 93
Baiyoke Tower II.. 93
Cabbages & Condoms 94
Vertigo Roof Top Restaurant 96
Grand China Princess Roof Top Bar 97

Michelin Star Restaurants 98
Nahm 98
J'aime 99
Vogue Lounge... 99

Bangkok After Dark 101
Soi Cowboy.. 102
Patpong.. 103
Nana Plaza... 105

- Nightclubs 107
  - Royal City Avenue (RCA) 107
  - Clubs on Sukhumvit 108
- Special Places and Odd Outings 109
  - Khaosan Road 109
  - The Slums of Khlong Toey 111
  - Inner-City Bike Rides 113
  - Museum of Death: Siriraj Medical Museum .. 113
  - Wang Saen Suk Hell Garden 115
  - Thai Boxing – Muay Thai 117
- Travel Tips 120
  - Traveling outside Bangkok 121
- Good to Know 124
  - Hospitals, Clinics, and Dentists 124
  - Travel Insurance 125
  - Traffic 126
  - Diseases and Dangerous Animals 127

Power Sockets and Electrical Wires 128

The Royal Thai Police 129

Final Thoughts 131

Asia Revealed Publishing Company

Preface

I have lived and worked in Bangkok for over ten years and I still find places that I did not know anything about. Furthermore, friends and colleagues always come back after the weekend with new recommendations of things to do and spots to explore. Bangkok is, in other words, inexhaustible, which obviously becomes a bit problematic when you might only have a few days to spend in the city. And considering that Bangkok is not even the main destination for many travelers to Thailand, there is a risk that this jewel among capitals is dismissed as nothing more than an annoying obstacle that must be endured on one's way to that cold drink on the beach.

If truth be told, I must admit that the most fun, interesting, exciting and – in some odd way – beautiful place in Thailand is indeed Bangkok. Here you can find just about everything. In a single day, it is possible to move from an enchanting temple, seemingly stuck in history and steeped in tradition, to the ultra-modern in some of the largest shopping centers in the whole of Southeast Asia. Or why not start off with an almost meditative boat trip around the forgotten river islands of Bangkok, and end the night with clubbing alongside the jetsetters of Thailand. As an added bonus, there are more green oases in Bangkok than you have time to explore – none of them of the same size as, for example,

Central Park in New York, however, large enough to make you fully forget the traffic mayhem of this sprawling city.

What is needed, though, and which I have noticed after frequent visits from family and friends, is a kind of short and concise, but nonetheless thorough, introduction to Bangkok to make the city more comprehensible. For the matter of fact is that everything in Bangkok comes in at least ten different versions at ten different locations, and to visit them all is something that, evidently, cannot be done even in ten years. Therefore, I have put together a compilation of "*the best of the best*", along with tips and advice about all those details that tend to cause problems when traveling in a foreign country. For example, how to go from the airport to the city in the most convenient way, what you should consider before getting into a taxi, the way the skytrain and the subway work, what you ought to do if injured or sick, and so on and so forth.

The book concludes with a section about practical matters such as travel insurances, hospitals, common illnesses, dangerous animals and general facts about Thai society, including important information regarding cultural codes, social rules and local taboos.

Asia Revealed Publishing Company

Arriving to Bangkok

Bangkok's main international airport is Suvarnabhumi. It is relatively modern with plenty of staff who one can ask for advice. However, it is occasionally not especially well staffed at passport control. And if you are unlucky, meaning that many international flights land at the same time, the visa process can take several hours. It is important to remember, though, that the immigration form handed out on the plane before landing has been correctly filled in. Otherwise there is a risk, if you encounter an overzealous inspector, that you are sent back to the end of the line.

After passing through passport control (check the visa stamp before leaving the area since it is difficult to change an incorrect one later on), bags and suitcases are collected from the baggage belts just behind the booths. Then, as in all other airports, you need to pass through Customs, which is located on the same floor. When stepping out into the Arrival Hall things will, however, become a bit more chaotic.

An advice for all newcomers to Bangkok: *do not be persuaded by unlicensed tour operators or taxi drivers to accompany them to their vehicles.* This is not only a very expensive option, but also one without any kind of supervision. All real travel agencies and tour guides at Suvarnabhumi Airport are registered and licensed, and their agents are *not* running around soliciting people. If you have booked a taxi, the driver will be waiting for you just outside the Arrival Hall, along the short promenade to the main area. If you have not booked a taxi, which is by no means necessary, there are several options available for getting into Bangkok.

Taxi

There are clear signs to the taxi stand and, as already mentioned, no licensed drivers are picking up customers inside the Arrival Hall. At the taxi stand, the passengers get a ticket from a ticket machine by themselves and then proceed to the designated car. The ticket received is also a reminder of the current airport taxi fee of 50 baht, paid by the passenger. When traveling by taxi, make sure that the driver turns on the taxi meter. A driver who does not turn on the taxi meter is planning to scam his passengers. In the taxi, there is information about the taxi driver and the car. And in case the taxi driver behaves in a strange manner, or refuses to turn on the taxi meter, it is advisable to jot down the information.

During the trip into Bangkok, which takes between 20 and 60 minutes depending on the destination, several tollways are passed and they are always paid by the passenger. Arriving at your hotel, do not forget that you also must pay the airport taxi fee of, currently, 50 baht. A tip is not expected, but it should be noted that the taxi drivers of Bangkok earn very little for their extremely long hours

Airport Limousine

You can book a slightly bigger car at the airport from one of the many tour operators who have their stalls marked as Limousine Services. A so-called limousine, though, is usually just a slightly nicer sedan, which will cost around 1 000 baht to central Bangkok. On the other hand, you do not have to pay for the tollways or the taxi fee of 50 baht. There are no additional fees when traveling by Airport Limousine. It is also worth noting that you pay per car, and not per passenger, meaning that there is money to be saved if sharing a vehicle.

Airport Rail Link

Bangkok's very comfortable skytrain has been extended all the way to the airport of Suvarnabhumi, making it possible to reach downtown Bangkok for just 50 baht. This is a very fast and efficient mode of transportation; if you are not towing around on a lot of luggage, since you probably have to continue the journey with another means of transportation to reach your specific hotel.

On the other hand, the Airport Rail Link stops at several stations that connect to Bangkok's other skytrain lines. Moreover, there is an abundance of taxis and tuk-tuks outside all skytrain and subway stations. And as long as you get off at the station closest to your hotel, the rest of the journey should proceed hassle-free.

Local Bus BMTA

The cheapest option for traveling into Bangkok proper are the public buses. There are, at the moment, five routes that begin and end at Suvarnabhumi. If going by bus, you should download a BMTA-map beforehand, which is a detailed description of all the fixed bus routes of Bangkok. The bus journey into Bangkok costs less than 40 baht, and all the buses stop near at least one or two skytrain or subway stations.

Public Van (minibus)

A competing mode of transportation are the minibuses, which do not only cross Bangkok from one side to another, but also entire Thailand. A minibus usually takes 10 to 14 passengers and a ticket costs around 40 baht per person. The minibuses from Suvarnabhumi stop at the main transfer hubs of Bangkok, where it is easy to change to public transportation.

<u>Coach</u>

There are several coaches that travel all over Thailand starting at Suvarnabhumi Airport. If Bangkok is not your end destination, this could be a viable option since it means that you do not have to make the extra journey to the bus terminals in town. All the coaches and their end destinations are listed on the website of Suvarnabhumi Airport, and you can book a ticket online.

***

NOTE: All the abovementioned options are clearly visible at the airport, and none of them deploy agents soliciting customers in the Arrival Hall.

If you have not booked a taxi in advance, just follow the signs to your chosen means of transportation, and ask the staff of Suvarnabhumi for help, if necessary.

Asia Revealed Publishing Company

Public Transportation in Bangkok

Getting around in Bangkok is fairly simple and straightforward; however, you often have to combine several different public or private modes of transportation to get where you want to go since the subway and skytrain only operate in certain areas of the city. Furthermore, it is worth noting that people drive on the left-hand side in Thailand. And do not trust traffic lights blindly. Many drivers in Bangkok have the bad habit of accelerating instead of slowing down when the lights switch, meaning that a handful of buses, cars, motorcycles, and tuk-tuks always pass at the very last second.

Skytrain and Subway

The skytrain (BTS) and the subway (MRT) are two modern and very convenient ways of getting around in Bangkok. The disadvantage, though, is that it is not always possible to find a station near one's end destination. On the other hand, there is always some kind of taxi service available at the exits of every station.

Skytrain

The skytrain is a raised railway track that mainly crosses Bangkok from the north to the south on two lines that connect at the downtown station of Siam (a third, as well as a fourth, line is under construction, and will open shortly). The stations on the two lines, the Sukhumvit Line and the Silom Line, are situated along the liveliest and most commercially developed areas of Bangkok, meaning that you often are forced to combine different means of transportation whenever you venture a bit off the beaten track.

Bangkok's skytrain is air-conditioned and easy to use with very regular departures. A single journey costs about 20 – 50 baht per person. The ticket is bought in a Ticket Vending Machine (TVM), where you press the button of the station you are going to, and then pay preferably with coins. A card is printed out, which you use to access the platforms. The card must also be used when leaving a station, meaning that you should not throw it away once you have got onto the train.

If you do not have coins for the TVM, you can get change from the staff at the ticket windows, who also sell different kinds of daily, weekly, and monthly travel cards. At busy stations, where many tourists and commuters pass, you can also buy single journey tickets from the manned ticket windows.

Subway

Bangkok's subway consists at the present of one single line, making it unusually easy to use. The clear disadvantage is, of course, that you hardly ever can get to your destination without combining at least two different means of transportation. On the other hand, the subway connects to the skytrain at several points in the city, facilitating quick and effective transfers.

On the subway, as is the case with Bangkok's skytrain, you must buy your ticket from a VTM. The subway ticket comes in the form of a small plastic coin, which is used to access the platforms. You need to save this token, since it is also used to exist the subway.

Express Boats on Chao Phraya River

One of the most interesting and, not least, cheapest means of transportation in Bangkok are the express boats, which run between the suburbs Nonthaburi in the north and Ratburana in the south. There are altogether three routes, although all of them traffic the same river. What separates them from each other are the piers they stop at, and this difference is signaled by colored flags attached to the boats on clearly visible spots.

The fastest boats, meaning that they only stop at the biggest and busiest piers, carry yellow or green flags. The second fastest, stopping at about every other pier, carry orange flags. And the slowest boats, which stop at every single pier on both sides of the river, do not carry any flags at all. For some tourist destinations, for example, the famous temple Wat Arun, the express boats are by far the fastest alternative. The cost of going by express boat is extremely low. And depending on the color of the flag, a single journey ticket can cost as little as 10 baht.

Canal Boats

The express boats travel up and down the river Chao Phraya, which divides old Bangkok on the western bank from new Bangkok on the eastern bank, while the canal boats cut solely through inner-city Bangkok on the eastern side. The boats travel along the big canal Khlong Saen Saep, stopping at many of the busiest places in central Bangkok. The canal boats might not represent the most convenient, effective, or even especially safe way of traveling in Bangkok, but undoubtedly one of the most exciting, as they pass local neighborhoods that otherwise would be concealed by skyscrapers and the never-ending flow of traffic. The fact is that the trip itself can become the activity of the day.

You usually pay for your ticket before getting seated, and it costs between 10 and 20 baht. Since it might be hard to know exactly where to get off, you might just as well pay for the most expensive one. The boats stop, however, at some spots where it is easy to continue traveling by other forms of public transportation. These piers are as follows: Thong Lo, Chit Lom, and Pratunam. The last mentioned is located near Siam, Bangkok's downtown. Getting off at the end station to the west is also recommended, as it is located in Rattanakosin, the Old City. Here you have easy access to many beautiful sights of the city, for example, the Royal Palace, the temples Wat Phra Kaew and Wat Pho, as well as the backpacker street of Khaosan Road (all these places will be presented in the following chapters).

It can, however, be a bit tricky to find the canal boats, since most of the piers are located behind some of the busiest streets in Bangkok. The easiest way is to ask the staff at your hotel where the closest pier is, but making sure that they understand that you are inquiring about the canal boats on Khlong Saen Saep, and not the larger express boats running up and down Chao Phraya river.

Ferry

At several of the piers used by the express boats, there are also ferry services. The trip only takes a few minutes, and does not cost more than a couple of baht, but at certain locations you can save yourself a lot of time. Besides, some tourist attractions might be hard to reach by any other form of public transportation. Wat Arun, also called the Temple of Dawn, located on the west bank of the Chao Phraya river, is one of them, as well as Museum of Death at Siriraj Hospital.

The easiest way to reach these "must-see" locations is to cross the river using the ferry services. Otherwise, you need to go by the bridges, and if you depart from your hotel during the wrong time of day, you might get stuck in traffic. In fact, most ferries are placed in the vicinity of the many bridges connecting old Bangkok with new Bangkok.

Buses

A very cheap but somewhat hot, and not very fast, alternative of getting around in Bangkok are the local buses, which come in many different forms and sizes. The buses are governed by BMTA, who also distribute a bus map with all the routes marked out. This map can be picked up at one of the larger bus terminals in Bangkok or, preferably, be downloaded from the Internet.

The buses come, as said, in various colors and with various numbers, and you have to make sure that the color and the number of the bus match. That is, a red non-air-conditioned bus on route 7 do not necessarily stop at the same places as a blue air-conditioned bus with the same route number. It is the sheer number of bus routes that makes it confusing, in addition to the fact that some of them only have their routes and stops printed in Thai. Nevertheless, they all run according to fixed time schedules, as in any other major city. And as long as you manage to find the right bus stop, there should not be any problems.

Once you have got on the bus, you normally pay to a conductor and not the driver. The cheapest buses will cost around 10 baht per single journey, and the most expensive ones will cost around 40 baht per single journey, making it an exceptionally cheap means of transportation. Always pay with coins or small bills since the conductor neither has time nor enough change to break a large banknote. Remember to keep the ticket, as there are ticket inspectors hopping on and off the buses of Bangkok.

When going by bus, you should avoid blocking the exits and offer your seat to the elderly, pregnant women, and young children since the rides are quite bumpy. When getting off, just push the stop button; however, it might be tricky to know exactly where you are in Bangkok when going by bus, and it is recommended to bring a map with you. Exploring the city by bus is an adventure in itself.

Asia Revealed Publishing Company

Taxis, Tuk-Tuks, and Motorcycles

Considering the size of Bangkok, there are certain areas of the city that cannot be reached by just using public transportation. Apart from the abovementioned travel alternatives, there are three other options, all with their respective share of pros and cons.

Taxis

Getting around in Bangkok by taxi is really simple, and most of the time you can flag one down at any place in the city. All the cars are clearly marked as taxis, although not uniform in brand, color or size, as is the case in, for example, London or New York. However, it is easy to spot the difference between a certified taxi and an unregistered driver.

One of the few issues that might arise when traveling by taxi is that the driver does not understand spoken English. Therefore, it is recommended to always bring a map with you, or perhaps a note with your destination written down. Another common problem is that the driver demands a fixed price. If this is the case, turn the driver away, and flag down another taxi, since it is always cheaper to be charged by taxi meter. This usually only occurs at large tourist attractions, in addition to some streets near big hotels.

A taxi ride in Bangkok should never cost more than a couple of hundred baht. On the other hand, the passenger is expected to pay the toll if opting to cross the city by the elevated Expressway.

Tuk-Tuks

A tuk-tuk is an iconic vehicle from Thailand in the form of a robust three-wheeler with enough room for a maximum of three passengers, although seeing far more people cramped into the limited space of the backseat of a tuk-tuk is a very common sight in Bangkok.

Tuk-tuks do not have any taxi meters and you always pay a fixed price. To avoid unnecessary problems, you should come to an agreement regarding the price *before* the trip starts. Tuk-tuks are generally a bit more expensive than taxis in Bangkok, on the other hand, they are somewhat faster, since they can avoid traffic jams by taking shortcuts through narrow backstreets and alleyways. Tuk-tuks are an excellent means of transportation for shorter distances in Bangkok. They should, however, be avoided if traveling far, since they do not come with any seatbelts. Moreover, if stuck in traffic, you are forced to breath in the exhaust fumes from other vehicles as you are sitting out in the open.

Tuk-tuks are usually found outside tourist attractions, and next to large shopping malls. They can, however, also be flagged down on the street.

Motorcycle Taxis

Motorcycle taxis can be found in more or less every street corner in Bangkok, and certified drivers always wear colorful vests with the name of the street they are working from printed on the back.

You pay a fixed price and, as is the case when going by tuk-tuk, you should always come to an agreement about the price before getting on the bike. At some motorcycle taxi stands, there are pricelists of trips to, for example, the nearest subway or skytrain station, as well as to other big and busy spots in the neighborhood. Motorcycle taxis are, though, really dangerous since drivers often ride between lanes to save time. Even so, they are the fastest and most suitable alternative within small city districts.

Asia Revealed Publishing Company

Exploring Bangkok

Finally, you have arrived at your hotel, often after a very long journey, and it is time to start exploring Bangkok. Since a city like Bangkok is utterly littered with big and small tourist attractions – and by listing them all, the length of this book would become impossible to handle – focus has been put on finding the best of the best in the most sought-after travel categories, in combination with odd and peculiar outings that you normally would not find in tourism-related materials online or in printed form.

All so-called recommended restaurants and hotels have, in addition, been excluded, unless they are part of a bigger tourist attraction, or stand out by being really quirky, original, or interesting. What the following chapters will present are the essentials of Bangkok. At the end of the book, there is a supplementary section with important information regarding everything from safety and travel insurances to advice on what to do in case of sickness or injury, in addition to central aspects of Thai culture and customs, including that all-important knowledge of the local dos and dont's.

Bangkok

Bangkok is a massive city. On the other hand, everything is relative, and as regards both population and area, there are many cities in Asia that are much bigger than Bangkok. Greater Tokyo, that is, Tokyo city along with all its surrounding suburbs, has a population of over 35 million. Bangkok city has only a population of 9 million. If you include all the suburbs, the number is roughly 14 to 15 million.

This is, however, not the whole truth since people moving to Bangkok from the countryside hardly ever change their addresses or tax registrations. Meaning that even though people are working and living in Bangkok, they are still registered in their old provinces and municipalities. In other words, there are far more people living in Bangkok than is shown in the system, making it impossible for the infrastructure to catch up. Simply put, it is hard to plan for streets, housing, schools, and hospitals when the total population keeps fluctuating. Moreover, both the illegal and the legal workforces from mainly the poorer parts of Laos, Burma, and Cambodia are not always included in the estimation of the total population of Bangkok.

Consequently, it is not surprising that the city of Bangkok feels, at times, as a rather chaotic and haphazard place. This, on the other hand, should not discourage anyone from exploring the parts of Bangkok that are off the beaten track since Bangkok is, statistically, one of the safest major cities to visit as a tourist.

The name Bangkok is, to many people's surprise, not the Thai name for the capital of Thailand, but rather what some of the first westerners to Bangkok came to call the city, which at the time was located on the west banks of the river Chao Phraya, in what today is known as Thonburi.

The word Bangkok is in fact an abbreviation of the words *Bang* and *Makok*, meaning something like "village of olives". The Thai name for Bangkok comes, on the other hand, in three different versions. The most common form is Krung Thep. The somewhat longer, and more formal, version is Krung Thep Mahanakhon. This is, though, a shortened form of the much more complicated original name, which is more or less impossible to get right in both writing and pronunciation. In fact, according to the Guinness Book of World Records, the Thai name of Bangkok is one of the longest names in the world. The meaning of Krung Thep Mahanakhon is, nevertheless, a summary of the original name, namely the City of Angels.

Before the end of the 18th century, the west side Thonburi was considered the capital of the country, but because of the volatile political situation with the war-prone neighbor Burma, the capital was relocated to the east side of the Chao Phraya river, Rattanakosin, and out of this enclave did the modern city of Bangkok emerge. Rattanakosin is still called "the Old City". However, although its historical significance, this part of Bangkok has in many respects been forgotten, which becomes very evident when considering that there are no subway or skytrain stations at all in the area.

Bangkok is divided into 50 districts called *keets*, and not until modern times have these districts been incorporated into a more detailed form of city planning. Up until the second half of the 20th century, the development of each respective *keet* expanded in a more organic fashion, where infrastructural solutions were not always put in the context of the entire city, not to mention the country. This has, in many respects, resulted in a complicated web of back alleys, lanes, and byways of so-called *sois* that haphazardly connect to one and another, as well as to many of the main roads crossing Bangkok.

However, whenever tourists speak about Bangkok, they tend to refer to the area of the city southeast of Rattanakosin (the Old City). The matter of fact is that large parts of Bangkok never ever see any tourists at all. Most of the tourism-related businesses, hotels, attractions, and destinations are located around or in the vicinity of the three major roads Silom Road, Sathorn

Road, and Sukhumvit Road. There are of course plenty of tourist attractions scattered all over greater Bangkok; nonetheless, the vast areas between these selected spots are, in most cases, completely ignored by visitors, especially Thonburi, along with other adjacent *keets* on the western side of the Chao Phraya river.

Contrary to many other major cities around the world, it is not easy to recommend a specific neighborhood to visit in Bangkok, as you might do when traveling to New York or London. The districts of Bangkok are simply too sprawled out and, not least, too hot to be explored on foot. In Bangkok, you usually need a specific destination in order to maneuver the city effectively. All first-time visitors to Bangkok are recommended to pick up a detailed street map from the hotel they have checked in to – all hotels have free street maps at their reception desks. Moreover, it is not associated with any kind of danger to be walking around with a big map in your hands, looking all disoriented and confused. This could be an invitation to robbery in many other capitals around the world. In Bangkok, though, it is an invitation to conversations.

Even so, there are a few areas in some *keets* where getting around by foot is actually the best way, namely China Town and Siam, both of which will be presented in the following sections and chapters.

Asia Revealed Publishing Company

China Town

One of the world's oldest and biggest China Towns is located in Bangkok. The neighborhood was established during the end of the 18th century, and has grown steadily ever since, resulting in a thought-provoking mixture of ancient Chinese culture and the Thai version of Buddhism.

The district is relatively big, but centered around the main street of Yaowarat Road, which could be your point of departure when exploring the area on foot. And on foot is the only possible way of accessing all the small and narrow lanes, back alleys, markets, and restaurants in the neighborhood.

There are no skytrain or subway stations in China Town, meaning that you have to travel here by some kind of taxi. The roads leading into China Town are, on the other hand, often clogged up by heavy traffic, and another route is recommended if heading towards the area in the afternoon. The most convenient way of reaching China Town is by taking the express boat to Ratchawong Pier. From here, you can walk up Ratchawong Road to Sampeng Lane and the main street of Yaowarat Road. Alternatively, you can take the subway to Hua Lamphong Station, which also is the central station of the national railway, and there flag down a taxi or tuk-tuk to cover the last little stretch into China Town proper. The distance between Hua Lamphong and China Town is, however, short enough for a brisk walk.

After dusk China Town undergoes a major transformation, most noticeable at Yaowarat Road, along with all the side streets connecting to it. From being a heavily trafficked hot spot of congestion, this central point of China Town changes into a food paradise, offering both traditional Thai and Chinese dishes, as well as all sorts of fusion food. To just stroll around in the neighborhood, ordering some dim sums here and a coconut ice-cream there, is an exciting little adventure in itself.

There are, however, a couple of attractions that you should not miss out on when coming here.

Tourist Destinations in China Town

China Town is open for business twenty-four hours a day, seven days a week. So, depending on when you show up, there are different things to do and see.

If entering China Town during the day, you should take the opportunity to visit, among other places, Wat Traimit, Wat Mangkol Kamalawat, The Thieves Market, and Sampeng Lane.

Temples in China Town

Wat Traimit, which is a traditional Thai Buddhist temple, is in the possession of one of the largest golden Buddha statues in the world. The temple is located at the outskirts of China Town and is a good starting point when exploring China Town. In addition, it is right next to the enormous Chinese Gate marking the outer boundaries of China Town. Similar gates can be found in more or less all China Towns around the world, but the one in Bangkok is, by far, one of the largest.

Another interesting temple, located in the middle of China Town, is Wat Mangkol Kamalawat. This temple, unlike Wat Traimit, is a temple steeped in Chinese traditions. That is, you will not only be able to enjoy intricate Buddhist adornments and decorations, but also stunning elements taken from Taoism and Confucianism.

Markets in China Town

Close to Yaowarat Road lies the Thieves Market, with the official name of Nakon Kasem. Here you will almost exclusively find second-hand goods. Since the merchandise sold is a blissful mix of bric-a-bracs from both western and Asian countries, the chance of stumbling across really interesting oddities is far greater at Nakon Kasem than at any other market in Bangkok.

It should be noted, though, that the current government (2017) is doing their best to rid the streets of unlicensed market stalls. Nevertheless, although the Thieves Market might not be as visible as it used to be, the character of the place still lingers on in the neighborhood. Not far from the sporadic corners of the Thieves Market lies another large shopping venue, namely Sampeng Lane, which is a long and narrow pathway that zigzags through the area, lined on both sides by cramped market stalls. Along this labyrinth of street vendors, all and nothing can be found.

If you are visiting China Town at night, you should proceed to Pak Klong Talad, also known as Bangkok Flower Market. This market is open twenty-four hours a day, but for some reason it is always busiest in the middle of the night. As the market is located right next to the pier at the Memorial Bridge, you have the opportunity to also visit the incredible temple of Wat Pho a bit further up the river. But since the temple closes in the afternoon, you should make sure that you visit the temple *before* the flower market of China Town. Besides, everything in China Town is more fun at night, not least because of the colorful lightings.

Asia Revealed Publishing Company

The River Chao Phraya

Something that might be called Bangkok's main artery is the river Chao Phraya, which originates several hundred kilometers north of Bangkok, among the streams, rivers, and creeks flowing down the mountains along the border to Laos. Chao Phraya has, in many respects, been the basis for the settlement that later became the city of Bangkok. Partly because of the water supply needed to grow rice, but also since the river makes it possible to access the sea.

On the west side lies Thonburi, and on the east side the part of Bangkok most people refer to when speaking about the capital of Thailand. Along this vital waterway, there is much to do and see, and some of the most stunning tourist attractions of Bangkok can be found here. In addition, going by boat on the Chao Phraya is one of the most comfortable and convenient ways of getting around in Bangkok, as long as the end destination lies within a kilometer or two of the pier.

Koh Kret

Chao Phraya has been widened and redirected several times during the last couple of hundred years and this led, sometime during the 18th century, to the creation of a small island in the middle of the waterway. This cut off piece of land came to be called Koh Kret. And on Koh Kret, it is as if time has stood still, which, not least, is noticeable through the culture and religion of the natives of Koh Kret.

Many of the inhabitants of Koh Kret belong to the ethnic group the Mon, who originate from Burma and came to be a large minority in Thailand over a thousand years ago. They are, as most ethnic groups in Thailand, Buddhists, but their version of Buddhism is slightly different from the one that you generally encounter in Thailand. A fact that is, for example, reflected by the temple architecture of the island. The Mon, in addition, has a long tradition of being skilled potters, and still to this day the people of Koh Kret engage in the craft of making and selling some of the best pottery in Thailand. A visit to Koh Kret is a quiet and relaxed affair. You do not come here to be entertained by the usual tourist-oriented activities, but rather to step into history and experience the way of life of old Bangkok.

The island does not cover more than a couple of square kilometers, and the best way of getting around is on foot or by bicycle, which can be rented on arrival. Another fun way of exploring the island is to hire a local boat, together with a captain, and go from bridge to bridge, and from pier to pier, stopping for a walk or a snack whenever you feel like it.

Getting to the actual island is, however, a bit trickier. The easiest way is to arrange the trip at a local travel agency, with transfer to and from your hotel. If you decide to go by yourself, there are two main ways of getting here. You can either flag down a taxi and drive to Wat Sanam Neu, a small community on the mainland next to the island, and from there cross over on a ferry. Alternatively, you could rent a private longtail boat from any of the larger piers along Chao Phraya river and head straight to the island. A longtail boat can carry up to twelve passengers, so even though the price is higher than for a taxi, you will be able to split the cost between more people. Besides, the actual trip in the longtail boat up the river to Koh Kret is well worth the extra cost, since you get the opportunity to not only enjoy the thrill of traveling in high speed on the Chao Phraya, but also to see some of the still very traditional housing communities along the river banks.

River Cruises

To venture up and down Chao Phraya during daytime by either the express boats or privately rented longtail boats is both fun and exciting. However, it is at night that the river really comes into its own. Unfortunately, though, most express boats end their services around 18.00. There is, however, a more extravagant alternative for anyone who wants to explore the river at night, namely luxurious dinner cruises.

Companies such as Chao Phraya Princess Cruise (there are, however, a multitude of serious tour operators in the market, all easily found by a quick search on the Internet) arrange trips after dusk where you, accompanied by good music and excellent food, can enjoy the very decorated and brightly lit City of Angels. The hotels, skyscrapers, temples, and bridges that line the river banks on both sides of the Chao Phraya are all illuminated by sparkling colored lights. And standing on deck, while taking in the vivid sight of Bangkok, is a truly dazzling experience.

Ayutthaya

Before modern Thailand was formed, the country consisted of a number of small kingdoms. One of them, just north of Bangkok, was called Ayutthaya, which still is the name of the city, and this historical settlement lies right next to the Chao Phraya river. To go to Ayutthaya by boat is an excursion that will take most of the day. In order to have enough time to explore all the unique temples and buildings of Ayutthaya, many of which have been put on the World Heritage List by UNESCO, you are recommended to spend at least one night in town.

In Ayutthaya, the architecture is very different from the one you will find in most other towns and cities around Thailand. Mainly due to the fact that during the time period that we in the West refer to as the Renaissance, Ayutthaya was the center of trade and commerce between the competing kingdoms of Burma and Cambodia, and there are still to this day many visible traces from the cultural influences of these two countries.

If you choose to travel up to Ayutthaya by boat, so that you will have the opportunity to absorb the rural side of northern Bangkok, there is the option of returning by taxi. If so, a visit to Ayutthaya can be done in a single day.

Asia Revealed Publishing Company

Parks in Bangkok

Bangkok is, to many people's surprise, a rather tidy and green city. Cleaning patrols are out and about every single night sweeping the pavements of dust and rubbish, there are hefty fines for littering, and you need a license to put up a market stall, start a restaurant, or engage in any kind of business activity in the public space. In addition, garbage trucks empty all the bins both regularly and carefully.

What can, however, cause a bit of a stench at certain places is the clogged-up drainage system, and you sometimes feel really nasty whiffs of bad air coming from some of the slightly open manholes. Moreover, even though the garbage trucks patrol the city every night, due to the heat it can start to smell of rotten food in some street corners, where the trash has been piled up to be carried away. But the fact remains that the trash in central Bangkok, and especially around commercial streets and lively neighborhoods, is removed swiftly and frequently, and the pavements washed clean on a daily basis.

Moreover, most Bangkokians take care of their own little slice of the sidewalk outside their shops or houses, resulting in the pleasant circumstance that you hardly ever come across cigarette butts, ice-cream wrappers, empty cans, or other waste products. On the other hand, the main roads leading out from Bangkok and, not least, major roads in general in Thailand, are littered with garbage, as many Thais have the bad habit of throwing their trash out of the car or bus windows.

Nevertheless, along most big streets in Bangkok, the city management has planted rows of bushes and trees to reflect the general tidiness of the capital, and nestled in among the crowded neighborhoods are pleasant parks of various sizes. To visit them all is not necessary; however, four of them stand out, two of which are located right in middle of the busiest streets of Bangkok.

Benjasiri Park

Benjasiri Park is easy to get to and lies right next to one of the most exclusive shopping malls in Bangkok, the Emporium. To get here, just get off the skytrain at Phrom Phong station on the Sukhumvit Line, and you will see the park from the platform.

Although rather small, Benjasiri is regarded by many as being the nicest park in Bangkok, and it is a genuinely lively place with a really exciting buzz about it. In many instances, the park has become a meeting place for culture and fitness activities. And while you can enjoy a classical concert in one end of the park, you can in another end play basketball or go skateboarding. There are also several big playgrounds for the kids in the area, as wells as a so-called daily Musical Fountain Show, in addition to two small outdoor gyms overlooking an artificial lake.

It is not, however, the facilities of the park that makes it stand out, but rather where it is located. Before 17.00, the park is more or less deserted due to the heat, but, as soon as the sun sets, the whole neighborhood around the skytrain station Phrom Phong comes alive. It is a genuinely modern metropolitan area with exclusive shops, restaurants of all sorts, commuters and business people hurdling along the busy pavements and streets, along with local families and foreign tourists.

Benjasiri Park is the center point of a truly buzzing corner of Bangkok.

Lumpini Park

The well-known park of Lumpini lies smack in the middle of Bangkok and offers a nice alternative to the usual big city attractions. The park is typically empty during the day due to the heat, but in the evening it literally explodes with people and activities.

Lumpini has among the Bangkokians become synonymous with health and exercise. In the huge park, there is a three-kilometer-long jogging trail, where an additional lane for bicycles has been constructed. You will also find a big outdoor gym in the park, which costs only a few baht to use, as well as a large number of public fitness machines laid out among the lawns in the form of a training track. In addition, there is a large swimming pool which, however, require a membership. This membership can, nonetheless, be sorted out quickly on the spot for an extremely low fee.

The most entertaining workout option is, though, the big aerobic sessions that spring up all around the park after sunset. Mobile stages and sound systems are erected and professional trainers hold dance inspired workout sessions for anyone who wishes to join. The children, on the other hand, can enjoy themselves at any of the many playgrounds. To top it all off, a large artificial lake is located in the middle of the park, filled to the brim with giant lizards, huge carps, and various turtles. Pedal boats for rent are available.

The easiest way to get to Lumpini Park is by skytrain or subway. If going by skytrain, get off at Sala Daeng on the Silom Line. If going by subway, get off at Silom or Lumpini.

Rot Fai Park

The third big park in Bangkok is Rot Fai Park (the official, but rarely used, name is Suan Wachira Benjathat). It is, however, called Rot Fai Park by the Bangkokians since a couple of old carriages are standing in the park, and the words *rot fai* mean train in Thai. This park is big with lots of shade under leafy trees and, because of that, absolutely perfect for picnics and bike rides. The bicycles can be rented in the park, and the cycle lanes are flat and easy to use. In addition, there are lots of various sport facilities, such as tennis courts and basketball courts, as well as a 25-meter-long swimming pool. Moreover, you will find an artificial lake in the middle of the park, which you can explore by going for a ride in a pedal boat. What makes Rot Fai Park the perhaps most interesting park is, though, the added bonus you get from its location, as well as all the activities going on in the vicinity.

At the far northern end of the park lies Bangkok Butterfly Garden and Insectarium, which is a wonderful series of greenhouses and plant collections filled with weird and beautiful butterflies and insects. At the other end of the park, you will find the Children's Discovery Museum. This museum, targeting all children with an interest in any branch of science, has been around for quite some time, but a couple of years back it underwent major renovations and is now of a high international standard, complemented with shallow pools and modern playgrounds. And if going to Rot Fai Park on a weekend, you should definitely take the opportunity to visit Chatuchak Weekend Market, which is one of the biggest markets in the whole of Southeast Asia.

The easiest way to get to Rot Fai Park, including Bangkok Butterfly Garden and Insectarium, Children's Discovery Museum, and Chatuchak Weekend Market, is by skytrain or subway. If traveling by skytrain, get off at the end station Mor Chit. If traveling by subway, get off at Chatuchak Station. All the abovementioned attractions are easily accessible from both these means of transportation.

Suan Luang Rama 9 Park

If getting tired of big city life, then a visit to Suan Luang Rama 9 Park could be something for you. This park is located in the east of Bangkok and occupies a truly massive area. Bear in mind, though, that Suan Luang Rama 9 Park closes its gates at 18.00, just when the other parks start getting busy. In addition, there is an entrance fee of 10 baht. The fee is collected since the park also functions as a kind of conservatory for international gardens from countries such as China, Morocco, England, and Italy, comprising of plants and adornments representing each respective culture and ecosystem. The yearly highlight is the Flowers Festival, which kicks off on the 1st of December, and ends on the 10th.

The park is so big that it takes several hours to walk all the way around it. There is, however, a miniature train crossing the huge lawns with stops at all the international gardens, and visitors are free to get on and off it as they please. Suan Luang Rama 9 Park is perfect for anyone who either has an interest in flowers and exotic plants, or who simply desires to switch off for a while and relax in a lusciously green space completely devoid of traffic and noise.

The easiest way to get to the park is by taxi. Alternatively, you could go by skytrain to Udomsuk Station on the Sukhumvit Line, and there flag down a tuk-tuk or taxi to cover the last few kilometers to the park.

Asia Revealed Publishing Company

Shopping Malls

Bangkok is a confusing conglomeration of streets of all forms and sizes, intersected by a couple of elevated expressways cutting through the center from south to north, and from east to west. The kind of meticulous city planning found in many major western cities has been, up to recently, fairly non-existent, and infrastructural problems have been solved when noticed. This has led to, among other things, that there is not just one city center in Bangkok, but several. The closest thing to a "downtown" there is in Bangkok is the area around the skytrain station Siam, where some of the largest shopping malls have been built. And it is, generally speaking, the shopping malls that have become each respective district's own local city center.

Many of the shopping malls in Bangkok belong to the same consortium, for example, Central Plaza or The Mall, meaning that most centers have a more or less identical selection of shops, restaurants, and entertainment venues. There are, however, a handful of shopping malls that have become so much more than just a collection of shops. Some of which are so interesting, and with such unusual designs and offerings, that a visit could easily be made to last the whole day.

MBK

The shopping center MBK is perhaps the most well-known mall in the whole of Thailand, and it has become something of an emblem of budget shopping. MBK resembles, in certain aspects, an enormous indoor market, spread out over eight air-conditioned floors. It is one of few shopping malls where you can, just as you would in a small local market, haggle about the price. There are several big chains present as well, selling brand names with fixed prices, nevertheless, a large portion of the area of MBK is occupied by very small shops, often not bigger than a spacious wardrobe, scattered all over the place in lane after lane after lane.

The floors at MBK are, to a certain extent, divided by the goods that are for sale. For example, on one floor, you will only find electrical products, and on another only clothes. This has not, though, stopped all the small shops from flowing into each other in a maze-like pattern. Just strolling around MBK is worth the visit, and the prices are markedly lower than the ones you will find in other more upscale department stores around Siam, which has contributed to MBK's immense popularity among the local population of Bangkok.

In addition, there are several food courts, restaurants, and cafes thrown out over mainly the bottom and top floors. Moreover, there is a large entertainment complex on the 8th floor with gaming arcades, modern cinemas, big bowling alleys, and a thrilling "Escape the Room" adventure with a really scary horror theme. There are two more "Escape the Room" venues in Bangkok, both of which are franchises of international companies of a very high standard. They can be found in the shopping malls Terminal 21/Interchange Building, at the skytrain station Asok, and Gateway Ekkamai at the skytrain station Ekkamai.

The main reason for visiting MBK, however, is not because of the entertainment section of this huge indoor market, but because of the cheap shopping and, not least, the general atmosphere. As an added bonus, it is very easy to access MBK: just get off at the skytrain station National Stadium on the Silom Line and cross the platform to MBK. Alternatively, get off at Siam and walk to MBK via the many footbridges.

Downtown Siam

Located around the skytrain station Siam, just a stone's throw from MBK, lie the shopping malls Siam Paragon, Siam Center, Siam World, and Central World. Together, they account for one of the largest shopping areas in the world. To top it off, they all are within walking distance of each other, and scattered along the streets between them is a myriad of small boutiques, shops, bars, restaurants, cinemas, and second-hand outlets.

These four shopping malls differ from MBK by being more luxurious, especially Siam Paragon. Here you can find the most lavish and expensive brand names for all walks of life. Strolling around in, for example, Siam Paragon is highly entertaining in a completely different way compared to MBK, as the trendiest and richest people of Bangkok tend to shop here. The experience becomes even more enticing at night when the whole neighborhood explodes in a cascade of bright lights and neon, creating the feeling of being in an extremely modern metropolis.

In all four shopping malls, there are excellent opportunities to experience the best of both Thai and western cuisines. Apart from exploring the shops and the many eateries, there are plenty of fun things to do for both young and old. For example, at Siam Paragon lies Sea Life Bangkok Ocean World, which is one of the biggest aquariums of Southeast Asia. And in the adjacent shopping mall, Siam Discovery, you will find a branch of Madame Tussauds.

In addition to enormous state-of-the-art cinemas and bowling alleys, there are also two really big and nice skating rinks in the area. The first one is located in Central World, and the second one in Siam Discovery. All necessary equipment can be rented on the spot, and in both malls skating lessons are offered for a couple of hundred baht per hour, making it an odd and fun thing to do considering the tropical heat outside.

The Emporium

The shopping mall the Emporium literally breaths luxury, in both form and substance. At this shopping Mecca, there are more or less only international brand names for sale. Right next to the shopping mall, in the adjacent building, lies the five-star hotel Emporium Suites by Chatrium. And the shopping mall is, in a sense, an extension of this truly high-end hotel. The Emporium has, simply put, been designed and executed on the basis of the clientele visiting the hotel, turning it into a beautiful oasis in the hectic inner-city of Bangkok.

This does not mean that you will not be able to find any cheap goods for sale here; however, the kind of mass-produced merchandise and odd trinkets that can be picked up at MBK have been sorted away. The collections of restaurants, cafes, and ice-cream parlors are, likewise, a reflection of the best the city has got to offer, with, of course, some cheaper western fast food alternatives thrown into the mix.

The Emporium does not only attract wealthy shoppers, but also everyday families, since there is an impressively large playland on one of the floors, as well an actual mini-farm with real animals that you can feed and touch. And on the top floors, you will find state-of-the-art entertainment zones, as well as ongoing fashion shows with regularly updated collections by new and upcoming designers.

The Emporium is easy to get to, and you can access the shopping complex from the skytrain station Phrom Phong on the Sukhumvit Line. As an added bonus, Benjasiri Park lies just next to it.

Terminal 21

The shopping mall Terminal 21, which is connected to the skytrain station Asok on the Sukhumvit Line, stands out for several reasons. First of all, due to the décor and styling of the place: the entrances of every floor have been designed according to the theme of airports, hence the name of the shopping mall. Once you have entered the various sections of this huge and imaginary airport, you are transported to different spots around the world. For example, on one floor you are visiting Paris, on another Istanbul, and on a third Tokyo. The idea is that you shop items, and eat foods, which are culturally specific to each respective place.

The end result is, of course, a rather haphazard mix of brand names, styles, and products. Nevertheless, the concept is interesting enough to make a trip to Terminal 21 something more than the usual run-of-the-mill shopping experience. In addition, in the adjacent building lies the Escape Hunt Experience, which is one of the best Escape the Room adventures in Bangkok, and only a stone's throw away you will find the notorious red-light district of Soi Cowboy.

Asiatique: The River Front

Not too far from downtown Bangkok lies the new outdoor riverfront shopping area The Asiatique, which is a truly large market space designed in a thoroughgoing retro spirit. The ambition has been to recreate the architecture of Bangkok in the early 1900s, as well as becoming one of the biggest shopping theme parks in the whole of Asia. And at the moment, there are over 1 500 shops and boutiques crammed together, along with over 40 restaurants, cafes, and wine clubs.

The shopping venues in this modern village is really varied. You will find both exclusive brand names and cheap products of the sort being sold at the throngs of market stalls in MBK or at Chatuchak Weekend Market. Furthermore, a lot of effort has gone into creating a wide range of entertaining shows for the visitors, such as the nationally well-known ladyboy cabaret Calypso Bangkok Theatre, the internationally recognized puppeteer Joe

Luis and his Traditional Thai Puppet Theatre, Muay Thai fights with skilled boxers, and a huge Ferris wheel overlooking the river Chao Phraya.

The Asiatique opens daily at 17.00, and closes around midnight. Although a bit outside central Bangkok, it can be accessed easily by the company's express boats running between the market place and the pier Sathorn, located right next to the skytrain station Saphan Taksin on the Silom Line.

Pantip Plaza

Pantip Plaza is not like any other shopping mall in Bangkok as you will only be able to find one kind of product for sale here, namely electric. It is a five-story-high Mecca for everyone who has got an interest in mobile phones, cameras, tablets, games, computers, or any other kind of device or appliance that can be hooked up to the Internet. Pantip Plaza is well-known far beyond the borders of Thailand, and many travel here to order all sorts of electronic products in bulk for resale in their own respective provinces or home countries.

Something that you should bear in mind, though, when visiting Pantip Plaza is that it is not always easy to spot pirated goods. And although the current government is cracking down on the trade in fake goods, there is still plenty enough in circulation. If you want to be absolutely sure that the product you buy is what it says it is, meaning that you will also be entitled to the stated warranty, you are better off visiting one of the bigger chains at Pantip Plaza, which are easily found among the throngs of indoor market stalls and small shops. In addition, at Pantip Plaza there are repair services offered for every device imaginable, usually at a very low cost.

Although relatively close to Bangkok's downtown at Siam, getting to Pantip Plaza is a bit tricky, since it does not lie right next to a skytrain or subway station. The best way is to flag down a taxi or a tuk-tuk.

Asia Revealed Publishing Company

Markets in Bangkok

Bangkok is, both in population and size, a very big city, especially considering that it does not ever really end, since the outer suburbs of Bangkok glide into the surrounding towns, for example, Chon Buri in the south and Rangsit in the north. This has led to numerous outdoor markets for the still steadily growing population. Quite a few of these markets have evolved during the years and transformed into some of Bangkok's most fun and entertaining tourist attractions.

The markets of Bangkok can, roughly speaking, be divided into three categories, namely street markets, floating markets, and night markets. As already mentioned, there are countless markets in Bangkok of all sorts – some, however, stand out, and should not be missed when visiting the city.

Chatuchak Weekend Market

The undoubtedly biggest market in Bangkok is Chatuchak Weekend Market, and as the name implies it is only open during the weekend, starting every Friday afternoon, and closing around 18.00 on both Saturday and Sunday. Once at the location, you need to keep a cool head, literally. More than 15 000 market stalls have been erected in what looks like an impenetrable maze of crowded lanes, and over 200 000 visitors scout the area for that perfect bargain on a normal weekend.

There is, nonetheless, some logic to the madness, and the vast space has been divided into sections according to the kind of goods they sell. The problem is, though, that after one or two turns you have completely lost track of where you are, which, on the other hand, is part of the charm of Chatuchak. Besides, the market is littered with small restaurants and cafés. And if you need to take a break, then just pop into any of them and order a cold drink to cool down. As always in similar environments, make sure that you keep track of your belongings, and bring enough cash with you since some of the vendors might not accept credit or debit cards. During night-time, the area is transformed yet again. All the market stalls are switched out to bars, restaurants, and clubs that keep the party going into the early hours of the morning.

The easiest way to get here is by subway or skytrain. If traveling by skytrain, get off at the end station Mor Chit on the Sukhumvit Line. If traveling by subway, get off at Chatuchak Park Station.

Pratunam Market

Pratunam Market is open both day and night. The matter of fact is that this market never closes, resulting in the interesting situation that the influx of customers, as well as the merchandise and services for sale, change during the hours of the day. However, a majority of the vendors at Pratunam Market sell clothes and fashion accessories, and among the stalls you will be able to find everything from cheap knock-offs to expensive brand names, as well as weird and bizarre costumes, high-end suits, and any fancy dress imaginable. The busiest time is from lunch until about ten o'clock in the evening. If you would like to experience the nightlife of Bangkok, without necessarily going clubbing or getting intoxicated, a visit to Pratunam Market is highly recommended.

As always in Thailand, there are plenty of restaurants, small bars, and cafes in the area. Large parts of the market are situated under raised roofs to block out the sun, some sections have spilled over into the adjacent streets and back alleys, and at the center of it all lies a five-story-high shopping mall.

The market area is located in central Bangkok, however, not right next to any subway or skytrain stations. The easiest way to get to Pratunam Market is, therefore, by some kind of taxi, and all the drivers of Bangkok are well-familiar with the place. As an added bonus, the market is not far from the tallest building in Bangkok, Baiyoke Tower.

Asia Revealed Publishing Company

Bo Bae Market

A somewhat more traditional street market in Bangkok, which, on the other hand, occupy just as much space as the above listed, is Bo Bae Market. This market is located between downtown Bangkok, which is centered around the skytrain station Siam, and the backpacker street of Khaosan Road. The easiest way to get here is by some kind of taxi.

The market itself is open from early morning to roughly six o'clock in the afternoon and is spread out between four bridges crossing the canal Phadung Krung Kasem. Right next to the market stand the tallest buildings in the area, Bo Bae Towers, clearly visible from miles away, and the market has merged with these towers occupying retail space on the first floors of each respective building.

Bo Bae Market is a genuinely hectic Thai-style market where both local and foreign traders in the textile industry come to buy mainly clothes in bulk. This is a place that is literally packed with people, market stalls, street restaurants, and everything else that you might expect to encounter at an enormous outdoor market in a proper Thai neighborhood in Bangkok.

Asia Revealed Publishing Company

Floating Markets

Many of the visitors to Bangkok mention that they have been to some kind of Floating Market. And while there are about a dozen markets of this sort in and around the capital, most of them are nothing more than really expensive tourist traps.

However, the ones listed below stand out for all the right reasons, and are highly recommended.

Damnoen Saduak Floating Market

The biggest Floating Market of them all, Damnoen Saduak Floating Market, is a beautiful and exciting spot on a river crowded with boats filled to the brim with merchandise for sale. However, since the market has, through the years, become a reflection of what tourists seem to be looking for, a large part of the local Thai customers has disappeared. But only from the central parts of the market. If you search out the peripheries of the market, you will still catch a glimpse of what Thailand looked like before the commercialization of the country really took off.

The drawback of Damnoen Saduak Floating Market is, nonetheless, the distance from Bangkok: nearly 100 kilometers. Meaning that most trips that are booked through local travel agencies are set really early in the morning. On the other hand, there is nothing stopping you from flagging down a taxi on the street to rent the driver for the day, which probably would be a bit cheaper than booking a trip where you are charged per person and not per vehicle.

Amphawa Floating Market

The second really large floating market around Bangkok is Amphawa Floating Market, which is, though, only open on Saturdays and Sundays. It lies somewhat closer to Bangkok than Damnoen Saduak Floating Market, and it is mainly to this market the Bangkokians go on the weekend. Already at noon, the area is utterly packed with people.

Contrary to Damnoen Saduak Floating Market, the market of Amphawa is so much more than just a somewhat different shopping venue with lots of local eateries. Along the canals of the floating market, there are several interesting and highly unique places to explore. It is recommended to rent a boat for a trip outside the actual floating market to visit some of the many spots of worship in the area, one being placed inside an enormous tree. Another fun activity is to go for a stroll along the edges of the canals to inspect the traditional architecture of the floating houses.

At Amphawa Floating Market, you can spend the whole day, and at night the entire area explodes in a cascade of lights and lanterns. Since the distance to Bangkok is shorter than that for Damnoen Saduak Floating Market, you can easily stay for dinner, and then head back to your hotel in a taxi whenever you feel like it.

Taling Chan Floating Market

If you want to experience a genuine floating market, but without wasting too much time on traveling back and forth, there is a smaller alternative just ten kilometers west of central Bangkok, namely Taling Chan Floating Market.

It is by no means as big as Damnoen Saduak Floating Market or Amphawa Floating Market; nevertheless, it is big enough to be called a floating market. In addition, it is a really traditional one with few tourists, meaning that you do not have to haggle about prices, or be too worried about pickpockets. Moreover, there are boats for hire taking customers for private trips up the river to see the local floating communities – a way of life that has existed in Bangkok for hundreds of years, but which, sadly enough, is coming to an end as the city is modernized

A trip to Taling Chan Floating Market can easily be combined with other excursions and activities on the same day. Taling Chan, however, is only open during the weekend, and it closes around dinnertime.

Asia Revealed Publishing Company

Night Markets

One of Bangkok's many characteristics are the local night markets that pop up here and there wherever you go. If coming across one by accident, just head into the narrow lanes of market stalls and explore the goods for sale, which usually are focused on clothes and food.

There are, however, four night markets that really stand out, and which can make up for an entire night out in town.

Khaosan Road

The perhaps most famous night market in Bangkok is not really a night market, but rather the alleys and backstreets in and around Khaosan Road west of central Bangkok. On the actual street of Khaosan Road, and all the various lanes and thoroughfares connecting to it, there are small shops open from early morning to late night. However, every square inch of the neighborhood is covered by markets stalls and mobile street vendors after sunset. It is a pure pleasure to stroll in and out of all the narrow alleyways to grab something to eat or haggle on a T-shirt or some kind of device. Everything under the sun can be found here, including all those things that you not necessarily would like to find!

Khaosan Road lies relatively close to the river Chao Phraya. If visiting Khaosan Road during daytime, you can take the express boat to the pier Phra Arthit, and from there walk to the almost as busy street of Soi Rambutrii. Once on Soi Rambutrii, the center of Khaosan Road is just around the corner. There are no skytrain or subway stations nearby, so the best way of getting to Khaosan Road at night is by taxi. However, when traveling back to your hotel, it is recommended to walk a bit outside the actual area of Khaosan to flag down a taxi. Otherwise, you run the risk of only meeting taxi drivers who are going to charge you a fixed and bloated price.

Patpong Night Market

In another part of town lies Bangkok's biggest red-light district, Patpong, which is easily accessible by skytrain and subway. The entrance of the main shopping lane of Patpong is located about 100 meters south of the skytrain station Sala Daeng on the Silom Line, and about 150 meters south of the subway station Silom.

As with Khaosan Road, the market is situated on a main thoroughfare, but nevertheless spills over to all the adjacent backstreets and alleyways. Patpong Night Market is a market that exclusively targets tourists, meaning that all set prices should be haggled down quite a bit. Most people visiting Patpong Night Market does not, however, do it just because of the shopping, but rather to experience the odd atmosphere that curtails this legendary and infamous corner of Bangkok.

There is no point in showing up before six or seven o'clock at night, since the neighborhood is more or less deserted during daytime. And when you do show up, be prepared. Due to the fact that the market is located within a red-light district, the streets are full of go-go-bars and scantily dressed waitresses.

Rot Fai Market

A night market that stands out for all the right reasons is Rot Fai Market. The words "*rot fai*" mean train in Thai, and Rot Fai Market of today used to be located smack in the middle of the railway tracks passing through northern Bangkok. This highly original market had to, unfortunately, close down in 2013 due to renovations of the tracks. However, instead of disappearing, it moved to eastern Bangkok. More accurately, Srinakarin Road soi 51, right behind the giant shopping mall Seacon Square, which is most easily reached by taxi. For obvious reasons, the authenticity of the market has vanished; nevertheless, it is still a piece of Bangkok history.

A somewhat smaller version of the Rot Fai Market, advertised as Ratchada Train Market, opened in 2015 on a much more central spot, namely behind the shopping mall The Esplanade, which is within walking distance of the subway station Thailand Cultural Centre. What make these two markets special is that they have put extra focus on art, retro, odd curiosities, and second-hand goods from all over the world. The atmosphere is genuinely nice and welcoming in both markets. But if you plan to stay out all night, then your best bet is Ratchada Train Market, since they also have a wide selection of bars and small scenes for local rock, pop, and folk music bands.

Rot Fai Market at Seacon Square is open from five o'clock in the afternoon to midnight every Thursday to Sunday. Ratchada Train Market is also only open from Thursday to Sunday, but closes much later. At both markets, but particularly at Ratchada, it is possible to party long into the morning hours.

Suan Lum Night Bazaar Ratchada

Suan Lum Night Bazaar Ratchada is a night market that brings together all the elements needed to have a fun night out with family or friends. Even though the actual market is huge, and consists of both an indoor and an outdoor section, the entertainment venues are at the focal point of every visit.

At Suan Lum Night Bazaar, you can enjoy live Thai boxing fights, free concerts, various traditional performances, as well as the Playhouse Ladyboy Show, which is a cabaret with only transsexuals, offering an extravagant show filled with both modern and classic show tunes. The night market, and all its venues, is complemented by a new five-star hotel, The Bazaar Hotel, with over 800 rooms.

The market is open daily, all year round, from about four o'clock in the afternoon to very late. The easiest way of getting here is by subway. The market area is within walking distance of the station Lad Prao.

Asia Revealed Publishing Company

A Bangkok for Children

At first glance, Bangkok does not seem to be a particularly child-friendly city. The entertainment venues are centered around restaurants, bars, nightclubs, shopping, and cultural excursions. But the matter of fact is that in and around Bangkok lie several large, exciting, and really fun tourist attractions that make for a perfect outing with the family.

The activities and places listed below are only a small selection of all that is available in Bangkok for the adventurous family. For a more comprehensive list of things to do with the family when holidaying in Thailand, the travel guide *Family Fun in Thailand*, published by Asia Revealed Publishing Company, is recommended.

Art in Paradise

Art in Paradise is a gallery with interactive 3D paintings; however, not in the form of holograms, but rather in the guise of actual paintings. What it is about is creating the illusion of the beholder stepping into the artwork. The paintings are huge, sometimes covering entire walls, and offer amazing photo opportunities where oneself becomes part of the motif. Next to most of the paintings, there are instructions on how you should position yourself to best create the impression of being an integral part of the composition. The optical illusions are stunning, and the whole family will be fascinated by the end result when captured by your own camera.

At the venue, there is also a brand-new multimedia room where the visitors can learn about, and experiment with, various creative forums. As an added bonus, a trip to Art in Paradise can easily be combined with other fun activities as it is located in the shopping center The Esplanade, which, among other things, can boast a huge state-of-the-art skating-rink. To get to Art in Paradise/The Esplanade, just take the subway to Thailand Cultural Center and exit the station to the north.

Bounce

Advanced and innovative trampoline parks are becoming more and more popular all around the world, including in Thailand, resulting in a company called Bounce setting up shop in two rather different shopping malls in Bangkok. However, Bounce in Thailand, which started out as trampoline park for mainly young people, has evolved into a fitness and adventure park that suits people of all ages and fitness levels. Besides massive and elaborate trampolines, there are now also impressive climbing walls and Adventure Challenge Courses, constructed according to the concept of the extremely popular TV show "Ninja Warrior". Even the fittest people will find parts of these courses truly challenging, making a visit to Bounce fun for both adults and children.

The easiest way to get to Bounce at the shopping mall The Street is by subway. Just get off at Thailand Cultural Centre and walk a couple of hundred meters north of the station. If visiting Bounce at The Emporium, get off the skytrain at Phrom Phong station on the Sukhumvit Line.

Dinosaur Planet

After several years of construction work, and with over 500 million baht invested, Dinosaur Planet opened its doors to the public for the first time in 2015. The aim had been to create the best edutainment place about dinosaurs in the whole of Southeast Asia. And on the premises, which is located in central Bangkok, the Thais' never-ending fascination of dinosaurs has now reach completely new levels. Here you will find a dinosaur museum, shows about dinosaurs, a so-called "Escape the Room" dinosaur adventure, a 4D movie about dinosaurs, and a giant dinosaur Ferris wheel, together with several other attractions that play with the dinosaur theme. You do not even have to be interested in dinosaurs to find it exciting and fun!

The easiest way to get to Dinosaur Planet is by skytrain. Just get off at Phrom Phong Station on the Sukhumvit Line. The park is located right next to the adjacent shopping mall The Emporium and Benjasiri Park. To get the most out of a visit, it is recommended to arrive sometime after 18.00.

Dream World

Just outside Bangkok's northern boundaries lies the suburb Rangsit, where you will find Dream World. This is an amusement park with many faces. On the one hand, there is the large funfair with merry-go-rounds, roller coasters, haunted houses, and log flumes. And on the other hand, there is the water park with a playground utterly drenched by spouting fountains.

What makes Dream World special is that the funfair and the water park have been combined with an entertaining mini zoo called the Animal Farm. Here visitors can get really close to the animals and enjoy fun-filled shows with healthy and well-trained cats, dogs, and horses. And do not miss the opportunity to step into the giant birdcage to feed the birds; myriads of small parrots that seem to be more interested in pinching people's ears than feeding on the snacks offered.

In the park, there also is a 4D movie theatre, in addition to several exciting shows. One of the more spectacular is Hollywood Action. In this show, the audience is invited to take part of the re-enactment of a live action movie. The guests can expect loud explosions, death defying stunts, fistfights, and everything else that comprises the makeup of an action-packed blockbuster. Dream World can also boast of having the first real Snow Town of Thailand, delivering an average temperature of 4 degrees below zero in an indoor landscape with actual snow. Warm clothes and sledges are included in the admission fee.

The easiest way to get to Dream World is by taxi. To shorten the taxi ride, you could go by skytrain to the end station Mor Chit on the Sukhumvit Line, or by subway to the station Phahon Yothin or Lat Phrao, and from there continue by tuk-tuk or taxi.

Dusit Zoo

Visiting a zoo in Asia can be an unpleasant and somewhat depressing experience. Animals in too small and dirty cages, inappropriate environments, uneducated staff, and too big of a focus on entertainment are some of the issues one might encounter. This, however, is not the case with Bangkok's largest zoo Dusit Zoo, which is under both state administration and Royal Protection.

The park is of a high standard and all the animals are healthy and well-fed.

Dusit Zoo offers a wide range of animal shows, for example, the Seal Show, where the audience is treated to many laughs and eye-catching tricks. Other fun and interesting activities include feeding barnyard animals and fishing for small sharks, but without any dangerous hooks. The rather vast area for sea living creatures and reptiles, spiders and snakes is also of a very high standard, offering a wide variety of both informative and entertaining displays.

At Dusit Zoo, you can hire bicycles to get around. There are also pedal boats available, in which you can explore the artificial lake with all its lizards, turtles and carps. A visit to Dusit Zoo is most fun during the weekend as there are more things to do then. The easiest way to get to Dusit Zoo is by taxi or tuk-tuk. The closest skytrain station is Phayatai on the Sukhumvit Line.

KidZania

A somewhat different excursion for the kids in Bangkok is a visit to KidZania in Paragon Shopping Center. KidZania is a miniature city on a rather grand scale. What makes the city of KidZania so unique is the fact that the children do not only play here, but actually try out all sorts of different occupations. In the city of KidZania, there is a multitude of jobs to choose between, and all of them have been constructed according to real life situations. The children are allowed to do everything that adults do in their respective job roles, and they also earn so called KidZania dollars from the work they put in. This money can then be used in a shop in the play city.

KidZania is relatively new and very elaborate. For the children it feels like "real work", especially when they get the opportunity to dress up like an actual pilot or perhaps doctor. Children that enter KidZania by themselves need to have some basic English skills to be able to understand the instructions. Younger children are welcome to participate in the company of an adult. There is, though, a small café in KidZania where parents can relax over a cup of coffee or tea while their kids explore the city.

The main target group is children between the ages of 4 and 14. If a child chooses to enter by himself or herself, the parents are required to leave a phone number where they can be contacted in case of an emergency. There are also routines in place for leaving KidZania so that no child wanders off by mistake. A visit to KidZania usually lasts for at least 3 to 4 hours, since there is so much to do, and so many jobs to try out. The easiest way to get to KidZania is by skytrain. Get off at the central station Siam and follow the signs to Paragon Shopping Center. KidZania is on the 5th floor.

Madame Tussauds

In Bangkok's downtown, which is centered around the skytrain station Siam, lies Madame Tussauds. Since this Madame Tussauds is a branch of Madame Tussauds in London, all the wax figures are of a standard that equals the ones in England. The figures are divided into nine categories, 1) Red Carpet Zone, 2) Music Zone, 3) History Zone, 4) Film Zone, 5) Leaders Zone, 6) Authentic History Zone, 7) Art & Science Zone, 8) TV Zone, and 9) Sports Zone. There are a couple of Asian stars in each category at Madame Tussauds in Bangkok that could be unknown to visitors from other parts of the world. Most of the figures, though, depict internationally famous men and women.

In addition, there are several interactive games at the location. You can, for example, play golf against Tiger Woods, or test your IQ against Albert Einstein. Due to the close proximity to the shopping center Paragon, visitors to Madame Tussauds have the opportunity to buy tickets to Sea Life Bangkok Ocean World at a greatly reduced price. Together, these two excursions take up most of the day. There are, however, plenty of restaurants and cafés scattered around the shopping malls where you can relax between the visits. The easiest way to get to Madame Tussauds is by skytrain. Get off at the central station Siam and follow the signs to the shopping mall Siam Discovery.

Safari World

Safari World is, like many other big entertainment venues in and outside Bangkok, a combination of several different kinds of parks. The main attraction is, though, an 8-kilometer-long tour through the safari park in either your own vehicle or in a shared pickup. During this trip, you will get the opportunity to see one of few feeding shows of lions and tigers in the world. In addition, English speaking guides join every tour.

Besides the safari tour, there is Marine World, where you can enjoy entertaining shows featuring dolphins and sea lions, among other animals. In an adjacent part of the park, River Safari World, you can ride log flumes through landscapes representing the jungles of Asia and Africa. In another section of Safari World, there is a long walking trail along several large animal enclosures, which connects to a giant birdcage where the visitors are allowed to feed the exotic birds. When visiting Safari World, you will also have the opportunity to go and see several entertaining stunt and cowboy shows.

The easiest way to get to Safari World, located in the northeast of greater Bangkok, is by first taking the skytrain to the end station Mor Chit on the Sukhumvit Line, and from there continue in a taxi.

Sea Life Bangkok Ocean World

On the ground floor of the huge shopping mall Paragon lies Sea Life Bangkok Ocean World, which is the biggest aquarium in the whole of Southeast Asia. Sea Life Bangkok Ocean World is the home of sea creatures ranging for the absolute smallest to some of the largest and most terrifying. Penguins, sting rays, sharks, and enormous freshwater fish can be observed through gigantic window walls offering panoramic views over lifelike underwater environments.

The most impressive part of the aquarium, though, is the long glass tunnel which is laid out below the bigger tanks of sea creatures. In some of the smaller tanks, you will find animals that are not as dangerous, but oh so much more terrifying, such as the enormous spider crab, the giant squid, and the fluorescent jellyfish. Several other activities are offered at Sea Life Bangkok Ocean World to make the visit more fun and exciting. Visitors can, for example, feed the animals from a small boat, which is visible to the guests walking through the glass tunnel underneath it. Moreover, there is the option of renting a specially designed diving suit for walks on the seabed to get really close to the stingrays and sharks. The newest addition to Sea Life Bangkok Ocean World is a 4D cinema. On the premises, you will also find a large play-ground for the younger kids in the family.

A trip to Sea Life Bangkok Ocean World can easily be combined with other fun activities in the area as it is located in downtown Siam. Just get off the skytrain at the central station Siam and follow the signs to the shopping mall Paragon.

Suan Siam Water Park/Siam Park City

In the northern outskirts of Bangkok lies the water and amusement park Siam Park City, also called Suan Siam Water Park. This really large park is divided into five zones – Water Park, X-Zone, Family World, Fantasy World, and Small World – targeting different age groups. For the teenagers and adults there are, among other things, log flumes and roller coasters of a high international standard, and for the younger kids a wide array of merry-go-rounds, rides, and games. It does not matter how old or young you are since everyone can find something exciting to do at Siam Park City.

About a third of the park is occupied by the Water Park. The Water Park itself is divided into many smaller areas centered around a big pool with a wave machine. Many of the smaller pools are connected to the waterslides in the area. Moreover, there is a several meter wide canal running through the zone and in which you can slowly and leisurely drift along the weak currents.

You do not have to visit both the Water Park and the Amusement Park at the same time, as guests have the option of only buying tickets for the zones they plan to use, which could save you a lot of money if visiting the park with really young children. The easiest way to get to Suan Siam Water Park is by taxi. Alternatively, you can get off the skytrain at the end station Mor Chit on the Sukhumvit Line, and from there continue in a tuk-tuk or taxi.

Asia Revealed Publishing Company

The Temples of Bangkok

Bangkok is a truly unique major city since it still has a very vibrant connection to its history and Buddhist heritage, and temples of all sizes keep popping up in the middle of all the markets, shopping malls, hotels, and skyscrapers lining the roads of Bangkok. To see them all is impossible; however, some of them stand out, and visiting at least one of the following temples should be considered mandatory if holidaying in Bangkok.

When entering a Buddhist temple, there are a couple of things, though, that you need to keep in mind. First and foremost, the way you dress. If dressed in too revealing of a fashion, meaning that the legs above the knees are showing, as well as displaying naked shoulders, there is a risk of being denied entry. You should also try to remember that most temples are not just places of worship, but also the place of accommodation for the monks, a fact that might be forgotten when moving around in throngs of camera-clad tourists. In other words, avoid being too loud, and make sure that all thrash goes in the bin.

A temple visit is usually most rewarding early in the morning – if showing up really early, there is a chance of meeting the monks when they are out asking for alms in the form of food. The food they receive during these rounds is supposed to be the only meal they eat during the day. If you are in Thailand on a national holiday, which is most likely since the Thai calendar is littered with public holidays, you should pay the neighborhood temple a visit. On the court yards, the monks usually arrange big markets, small funfairs, and sometimes even concerts with both traditional musicians and local pop stars.

Wat Arun: Temple of Dawn

As is the case with most temples in Thailand, Wat Arun is only open during the day. It is recommended, though, to somehow pass it at night since it is lit up as a torch spreading a golden light over the river. Wat Arun is located on the west side of the Chao Phraya river and the easiest way to get here is by boat, departing from Sathorn pier, right next to the skytrain station Saphan Taksin on the Silom Line. All express boats do not stop at the right pier, so make sure that you mention that your final destination is Wat Arun at pier 8 before buying a ticket. When arriving at pier 8, which is on the east side of the river, you need to cross over to the other bank by the ferry service, which costs close to nothing, and does not take more than a minute or two.

Wat Arun is markedly different from all other temples in Thailand. The architecture is truly unique and the temple rises from the river in the form of a giant scepter.

The walls of this seventy-meter-high tower are dressed in porcelain and colored glass, and people came from all over Thailand during the 1800s to donate plates, cups, bowls, and glasses in order to finish the magnificent construction.

Along the colorful cladding of the surface, there are stairs that will take you close to the top, where you will be rewarded with a breath-taking view of the river. In case the steps are too challenging, but you still want to enjoy the stunning sight of Wat Arun, you are recommended to have dinner at any of the restaurants along the riverfront at night. Because when the sun sets, and all the lights attached to the leaning walls of Wat Arun are turned on, it truly feels like stepping into a perfectly arranged postcard.

The Grand Palace and Wat Phra Kaew

When traveling to Bangkok, you should not miss out on a visit to the Grand Palace and Wat Phra Kaew, also called the Temple of the Emerald Buddha. The temple is actually located within the palace walls, making it possible to explore them both at the same time – although the Grand Palace is still used when greeting foreign dignities, or conducting important ceremonies, no one in the Royal Family lives there anymore.

The design of the Grand Palace is truly remarkable and several of the buildings show discernible traces of European architecture. When visiting, you are free to roam around the royal premises relatively uninterrupted, and inside the courtyards you will find Thailand's most important temple, Wat Phra Kaew. Moreover, in Wat Phra Kaew rests one of Thailand's most sacred relics, the Emerald Buddha, which is a Buddha statue that has been cut out of one single block of jade. This statue constitutes an integral part of a very important ritual that is performed three times a year and which can only be officiated by someone in the Royal Family – the ceremony is carried out in conjunction with the shifting of seasons in order to bless the country in the forthcoming year.

Another aspect of Wat Phra Kaew, separating it from other temples in Thailand, is the fact that no monks or nuns live on the premises. At Wat Phra Kaew, you will also find a scale model of another important temple in this part of the world, namely the World Heritage temple of Angor Wat in Cambodia, clearly marking the two countries' shared religion and history – a somewhat violent past that has pushed the border between Thailand and Cambodia both to the west and to the east in turns during the centuries.

At Wat Phra Kaew, there are guided tours available between 10.00 and 14.00, with complimentary Personal

Audio Guides (PAGs) in the languages of English, German, French, Spanish, Russian, and Chinese. The Grand Palace and Wat Phra Kaew are located in the city district of Rattanakosin, within walking distance of the river Chao Phraya, but not close to any subway or skytrain stations. The easiest way to get here is by boat. On the other hand, the palace can be accessed easily from most parts of the city by any form of taxi, and there is absolutely no need to arrange a visit through a local travel agency.

Contrary to the practice of most other temples in Thailand, there is an admission fee for the Grand Palace and Wat Phra Kaew, currently at around 400 baht per person. In addition, the dress code is a bit stricter. However, if wearing too little, there is the possibility of borrowing clothes on site against a small deposit. Furthermore, the opening hours also differ a bit from other temples around Thailand. At the Grand Palace and Wat Phra Kaew, they close as early as 15.30.

Wat Pho: Temple of the Reclining Buddha

The third big temple in Bangkok that is well worth a visit is Wat Pho, also located in the district of Rattanakosin, about one kilometer south of the Grand Palace and Wat Phra Kaew. In addition, within walking distance of the express boats on the river Chao Phraya.

What makes Wat Pho unique is its enormous reclining Buddha statue, completely covered in gold foil. It is a massive 46 meters long and 15 meters high, so big that it fills out an entire hall. Apart from this impressive statue, there are a number of smaller Buddha statues also covered in gold foil lining the many corridors and halls of the premises. The area of Wat Pho is not as vast as Wat Phra Kaew, however, fewer tourist are drawn here, making it feel less crowded. Nonetheless, there are tours to join with English speaking guides. And to make the visit more entertaining, you are recommended to buy a bowl of coins that you drop in 108 ornamented bronze containers for good luck. Another unique aspect of Wat Pho is the fact that the temple is the center of a very special style of massage therapy. So, after having explored all the rooms, halls, and courtyards, why not visit the massage parlor to enjoy a relatively unusual form of massage, which includes some features of Yoga.

The entrance fee to Wat Pho is 100 baht, and it closes a couple of hours later than the Grand Palace and Wat Phra Kaew, making it possible to visit them both in one and the same day.

Asia Revealed Publishing Company

Unusual and Unique Restaurants

In Bangkok, there is an abundance of restaurants, and you often hear people saying that *"one half of the population cooks for the other half"*. In many cases, the food offered at all these restaurants is pretty similar. Of course, there are better and worse outlets, but what makes a restaurant the main destination on a day out in town does not necessarily have anything to do with the food served, unless we are talking about Michelin Star Restaurants.

Below follows a couple of restaurants that you might want to visit if you are looking for something more than just a plate of good food.

Baiyoke Tower II

In central Bangkok, relatively close to Siam, lies the capital's second tallest building, Baiyoke Tower II. The skyscraper is 88 stories high and has been divided into various zones. For the meagre sum of around 300 to 500 baht, you are allowed to access them all. There is a spinning deck on the 84th floor where visitors can view the city in all four directions, and on the 77th floor you will find a Skywalk with enormous panoramic windows and powerful binoculars. Moreover, a large shopping mall has been squeezed in on the floors directly beneath it.

The restaurants available are, in addition, very good, and some belong to the four-star hotel in the building. Many of the restaurants on the upper floors are various buffets. Furthermore, a Floating Market has been set up on the 75th floor, complete with traditional Thai dishes and decorations. It might sound a bit strange to create a floating market at the top of a skyscraper, and although the end result is somewhat cheesy, it still definitely adds to the overall experience of Baiyoke Tower II. As an added bonus, visitors are allowed to use the spa of the hotel for a small fee.

Getting to Baiyoke Tower II, situated on Ratchaprarob soi 3, by public transportation requires a rather long walk from the closest skytrain station Chit Lom or Ratchatewi. The easiest way of getting here is therefore by taxi.

Cabbages & Condoms

One of the quirkiest restaurants in Bangkok is Cabbages & Condoms with its absurd slogan: *"Our food is guaranteed not to cause pregnancy."*

Cabbages & Condoms, which has now evolved into a national chain of restaurants, was originally started by an ex-politician who thought that more had to be done about the social problems of Bangkok. Some of these overarching issues are handled by the organization Population and Community Development Association (PDA), which, among other things, work with family planning, unexpected pregnancies, and sexually transmitted diseases. To openly talk about sex in Thailand is still somewhat of a taboo, especially when it comes to teenagers, resulting in a statistically high frequency of teenage pregnancies. Cabbages & Condoms is part of breaking these taboos, and some of their profits go to the organization PDA to help them in their work.

At Cabbages & Condoms they serve both international and national dishes of a very high standard. However, this establishment is just as much a mellow cocktail bar as it is a restaurant. Nonetheless, it is not really the food, nor the drinks, that is the lure of the restaurant, but rather the extremely unusual décor, which unabashedly promotes the use of condoms. All around the very pretty restaurant – at nighttime, the whole area comes to life by thousands of lights – there are mannequins dressed in clothes entirely made out of condoms. These absurd furnishings are complemented by a small waterfall in the background and a band playing traditional music on traditional instruments.

Cabbages & Condoms lies in central Bangkok on Sukhumvit soi 12, which is within walking distance of the subway station Sukhumvit, as well as the skytrain station Asok.

Asia Revealed Publishing Company

Vertigo Roof Top Restaurant

Many of the most interesting and luxurious restaurants are located in five-star hotels. This is also the case with Vertigo Roof Top Restaurant – a restaurant that has taken the concept of Roof Top Restaurant to new dizzying heights.

The hotel Banyan Tree Hotel lies in the business district of Sathorn on South Sathorn Road, within walking distance of the subway station Lumpini, and the skytrain station Chong Nonsi. On the other hand, walking distance in Bangkok can, at times, feel both sweaty and weirdly long, and the most comfortable way of getting to Banyan Tree Hotel is by taxi. Especially since their dress code demands some kind of a formal outfit. That is, no flip-flops, shorts, or T-shirts.

The building is one of the tallest in Bangkok and Vertigo Roof Top Restaurant is on the 62nd floor. What separates Vertigo from other Roof Top Restaurants is the fact that the restaurant is not placed indoors, but rather is out in the open with just a thin glass barrier between the guests and the hard pavement 200 meters down. This means, of course, that the opening hours are dependent on the weather. On rainy days, you have to suffice with the indoor restaurant. However, when it is open, a visit to Vertigo is truly something out of the ordinary, boasting a complex menu and drink list that match the exclusivity of the restaurant.

For anyone who desires to exchange the heat of Bangkok for luxury and cool winds on the 62nd floor, this is a must.

Grand China Princess Roof Top Bar

A far cheaper, and more relaxed, option to five-star Vertigo is the revolving bar on the roof top of the hotel Grand China Princess. This bar and restaurant lies in the middle of China Town and is a perfect complement to the busy and somewhat chaotic street life of the area. Here you can take a break from all the sounds, smells, and sights of the very interesting and intense district of China Town, which is located in and around Yaowarat Road.

It takes the bar two hours to complete a full circle, allowing you to enjoy the view in all four directions during dinner. The bar opens at 17.00, but, as is the case with all roof top bars and restaurants in Bangkok, to fully appreciate the skyline of the city, a visit to Grand China Princess is best around sunset. After dinner or cocktails, you are recommended to venture out into China Town again to experience how it comes to life after dark.

Asia Revealed Publishing Company

Michelin Star Restaurants

Bangkok is a modern and international major city, attracting people from all over the world. This has, in recent years, led to the establishment of several Michelin Star restaurants by internationally acclaimed chefs.

If you are looking for something over and beyond the usual evening meal, regardless of what kind of cuisine you fancy, then a visit to any of the three restaurants mentioned below is recommended.

Nahm

The head chef at Nahm Restaurant is the Australian David Thomson, who was the first chef ever to be awarded a Michelin Star for cooking Thai food.

Nahm, which is located at the hotel COMO Metropolitan Bangkok at South Sathorn Road, reasonably close to the skytrain station Chong Nonsi and the subway station Lumpini, is year after year voted as one of the best restaurants in the world serving Thai food.

What makes the food at Nahm so special is that the menu does not only consist of highly complex dishes, but also of a wide array of so-called street foods. However, with a truly refined touch.

J'aime

The chef Jean-Michel Lorain has been awarded three Michelin stars throughout the years, and when he opened his restaurant J'aime at the hotel U at Sathorn it soon became the most prestigious one in the whole of Bangkok.

Jean-Michel Lorain has his roots in France, and his Bangkok venue is an absolute must for anyone who has grown tired of the Thai cuisine. The food at J'aime is at its core French, although modernized and with many influences from around the world. The menu is, in many respects, a reflection of the menu in Jean Michel Lorain's Michelin restaurant in Burgundy, France.

J'aime is located in Soi Ngam Duphli, within walking distance of the subway station Lumpini. However, free transfer can be arranged when booking a table.

Vogue Lounge

Vogue Lounge started as a bar, but quickly came to be one of Bangkok's trendiest and most discussed restaurants. The menu is compiled by head chef Vincent Thierry, who has been awarded two Michelin stars. The dishes consist of an international mix of the best from the most classic cuisines around the world. But the food is not the only reason to visit Vogue Lounge. The exclusive bar is just as prominent as the restaurant, and it is open long into the night.

Getting to Vogue Lounge is really easy as the restaurant lies just around the corner from the skytrain station Chong Nonsi on the Silom Line.

Asia Revealed Publishing Company

Bangkok After Dark

Most people visiting Bangkok are well aware of the fact that there are several big red-light districts in the city, which, in a way, is a bit surprising since the laws regulating the sex trade are fairly similar to the laws found in some of the stricter countries of Europe. On the other hand, there exists a long tradition in Thailand of men having mistresses, and several surveys have found that the majority of customers to brothels in Thailand are in fact Thai men. Nevertheless, the part of the sex industry that targets foreign tourists is so much more visible than the one catering to the locals, and it is the tourist-related red-light districts that most often figure in mass media reports.

A circumstance that further complicates the picture is the fact that the sex industry has come to constitute a large part of Thailand's shadow economy, and the money generated does not only end up in the pockets of bribed officials, pimps, bargirls and prostitutes, but it also travels back to the poor rural population. The Thai attitude towards the sex industry is in many respects a mirroring of the lack of social welfare, as there is no real financial assistance to access, for example, sufficient state pensions or child benefits. The laws governing the sex industry are therefore hardly ever implemented, since that would tip the scale and force a change to the core economics of the country. Consequently, everyone visiting Thailand must make up his or her own mind of what is acceptable and unacceptable.

It needs to be pointed out, though, that many of these red-light districts also function as completely normal tourist attractions in the form of street markets, food courts, nightclubs, and beer bars. Meaning that one should be cautious about making any sweeping generalizations.

Soi Cowboy

Soi Cowboy, which is within walking distance of the skytrain station Asok on the Sukhumvit Line, right next to the huge shopping mall Terminal 21, is relatively descent, despite all its go-go-bars. Along the street, cutting through this infamous neighborhood, there are numerous scantily dressed barkers trying to lure customers into the bars. They are, however, not overly pushy, and you could even say quite polite compared to barkers at similar tourist spots around the world.

Inside the go-go-bars, there are usually one or two stages where topless women, sometimes completely naked women, dance. Hostesses offer their company, and the customers are expected to buy them drinks, which they get a commission on from the owner of the bar. At Soi Cowboy, there will be fixed prices on the drink lists, clearly displayed to the customers. There are no entrance fees and, considering it is a red-light district well-established in the sex industry of Bangkok, the risk of getting into trouble, or being scammed, is fairly low.

The sale of sexual services is, in addition, carried out in the background. And it is possible to avoid it altogether if you are only looking for some good live bands, relatively cheap drinks, and dance shows with topless women.

Patpong

Patpong, which used to be the worst and most depraved red-light district in the whole of Southeast Asia, has during the last couple of years become much tidier, safer, and more tourism-oriented, which does not mean that all the shows of the past have disappeared – the term "ping pong show" was coined at Patpong, and yet today it is possible to find weird performances where naked women use their genitals to pop balloons with inserted blowpipes. It is, needless to say, at these establishments that tourists run the greatest risk of getting into trouble.

As a rule of thumb at Patpong, everything that is located at street level, regardless of content, is regulated and safe, while everything that takes place in shady bars on the second or third floor of the buildings, and to which visitors are only granted access by low-key barkers, are dodgy hangouts where you most likely will be scammed. A common way of practice is that only a couple of guests are let in at a time. And once seated, the doors are locked and no one is allowed to leave until the extremely bloated bar bills have been paid in full.

Patpong is, in addition, also the biggest scene for Bangkok's many transvestites and transsexuals, who are commonly referred to as Ladyboys. As is the case with prostitution, go-go-bars, striptease shows, and the sex industry in general in Thailand, many moral and macroeconomic questions and issues are brought to the limelight at Patpong. And at the end of the day, responsibility lies in the hand of the beholder, since the laws governing this part of Thai society are not implemented at all.

On the other hand, as already mentioned, the neighborhood of Patpong has become cleaner, in all aspects, and nowadays there are both CCTV and tourist police officers present, making it a safe place with the exception of pickpockets. Moreover, Patpong lies right next to a huge night market, several western restaurants and fast food joints, franchise sports bars, small shopping malls, language schools, offices, banks, and all sorts of other commercial outlets. The sex scene of Patpong is just one component of this bustling and busy neighborhood.

Getting to Patpong is really easy: just get off the skytrain at Sala Daeng station on the Silom Line, or at Silom station if traveling by subway.

Nana Plaza

Within walking distance of the skytrain station Nana on the Sukhumvit Line lies Nana Plaza. In contrast to Soi Cowboy and Patpong, this red-light district does not attract tourists who, for one reason or another, have let curiosity take the upper hand, but rather single men looking for prostitutes.

At both Patpong and Soi Cowboy, there is a vibrant music scene with many good live bands, in addition to markets and western restaurants and sport bars. At Nana Plaza, though, it is the sex theme that is the undisputed core of the establishments in the area, making the so-called barkers much pushier and more straight forward. The prostitutes do not, as in the other places, work in the background, but operate openly and market their services without sugar-coating it.

At Nana Plaza, you simple cannot miss what it is all about. Neither is it an area that you would wander into by mistake since the bars, the neon lights, and the looks of the service staff, as well as the clientele, clearly and unabashedly state what you can expect to find. Strangely enough, though, Nana Plaza is located right next to several four and five-star hotels, along with other upscale venues. During daytime, it more or less disappears into its surroundings. However, as soon as night falls, this block takes center stage.

Asia Revealed Publishing Company

Nightclubs

Most people that travel to Bangkok plan to visit the temples, explore the culture, relish in all the good food, go shopping at local markets, or indulge in a bit of luxury at the extremely cheap four and five-star hotels. However, Bangkok is also the center of a very intense nightclub scene, which is not at all about the usual beer gardens and go-go-bars that you hear so much about.

In many respects, Bangkok is the New York of Southeast Asia. And in contrast to other major cities in the neighboring countries, in Bangkok you do not have to wait until the weekend to party hard. Whenever you wish to go clubbing, there are several exiting places to choose between.

Royal City Avenue (RCA)

The best nightclubs are in an area called Royal City Avenue (RCA). This vast venue, consisting of a whole block of various nightclubs, is governed under a special set of rules, meaning that you can continue partying at RCA long after other places around town have closed for the night. The main street is littered with bars and clubs playing anything from hip-hop and EMD to drum n' bass, dance, and house. Some of the best are Route 66, Onyx, and the Tha Beatlounge.

At the larger clubs, it is not unusual to spot internationally recognized DJs. The clientele consists mainly of a mix of wealthy and hip Thais and expats living in Bangkok. Tourists wearing flipflops and beach shorts run the risk of being denied entry. RCA is located between the subway stations Phra Ram 9 and Petchaburi. It is, however, a bit too far to walk, and the easiest way to get here is by taxi.

Clubs on Sukhumvit

In addition to the many nightclubs around RCA, there are several other venues which, more often than not, can boast of having both internationally and nationally recognized DJs playing. Many of them can be found along Sukhumvit Road. On the other hand, Sukhumvit is an extremely long road, and it is definitely not possible to crab a taxi to an unspecified location at Sukhumvit and then start strolling around looking for a club or two.

However, just mention the number of the *soi* you are going to, and the taxi driver will most likely find the club. Some of the best at Sukhumvit are as follows: Levels Club & Lounge at soi 11, Sugar at soi 11, Insanity at soi 12, Glow at soi 23, Sing-Sing Theatre at soi 45, Grease Nightclub at soi 49, and Beam Nightclub at soi 55.

Asia Revealed Publishing Company

Special Places and Odd Outings

In Bangkok, there are a handful of places and outings that are so unique, or perhaps weird, that you really should do your best to experience at least one or two of them.

Khaosan Road

This road, or, more accurately, this block, is something you either hate or love. Up until the 1980s, the neighborhood was not that different from all the other somewhat poorer parts of western Bangkok (the fact is that there still is not enough going on financially to justify extending the subway or skytrain to the district). But then, out of the blue, Khaosan Road started to attract backpackers from all over the world, and once the ball had been set in motion, the evolution of Khaosan Road could not be stopped.

Hostels, low budget hotels, mini travel agencies, bars, and street food restaurants mushroomed as the word about Khaosan Road was spread around the world, turning it into a hub for backpackers traveling through Southeast Asia. This transformed Khaosan Road and the connecting backstreets and alleyways to a genuinely international and multicultural melting pot of everything under the sun. By just strolling down the street, you will be able to pick out at least twenty different languages. And for anyone who is eager to quickly move on to, for example, a southern island, a northern mountain town, or a neighboring country, this is the place to be: in every other street corner lie small travel agencies, ready to whip up a charted VIP bus or a fast minivan for immediate departures to anywhere around Southeast Asia.

Khaosan Road became even more talked-about after the author Alex Garland released his novel *The Beach*, 1996, which later on was filmed with Leonardo DiCaprio as the leading actor. The years that followed saw an unprecedented growth of small businesses along the street, and the backpacker chaos spilled over to the adjacent block of Soi Rambutrii. In both these places, you can find backpackers that have been around for weeks, even months. People who arrived on their way to another destination, but got stuck in a kind of warped sense of reality.

There is a police station in one end of Khaosan Road, but the officers do not seem to be particularly interested in what is going on in and around the block, with the exception of making sure that violent crimes, thefts, and drug abuse keep to a minimum. Khaosan Road is open for business 24 hours a day, 7 days a week, all year round.

Asia Revealed Publishing Company

The Slums of Khlong Toey

Most tours that can be booked on the web or in Bangkok take their customers to the same list of places, and in many cases it is a waste of money, since all major tourist attractions in Bangkok are very easy to access by oneself. On the other hand, there are certain parts of Bangkok that can be a bit tricky to explore without an accompanying guide. In addition, there are numerous interesting places scattered around town that you cannot even know anything about without first getting an inside tip. Some of the most interesting tours available take you to what might be called the "real Bangkok". In other words, parts of the city that do not have anything to do with tourism or big money.

In central Bangkok lies the district of Khlong Toey. This district is very large, both in size and population, and some areas of it can be found in the most tourist exploited streets of the city, for example, Sukhumvit soi 20, 22, and 24. But Khlong Toey is also the home of Bangkok's largest slum. The authorities are not sure of how many people actually live in the slums of Khlong Toey, as there is no accurate national registration of this part of Bangkok. Moreover, the local population has partially been mixed up with unregistered immigrant workers from Laos, Cambodia, and Burma.

In contrast to slum areas in other major cities around the world, the slums of Khlong Toey are relatively safe, which has led to the development of guided tours through the cramped tin-roofed alleys of slum dwellings. The amount of tours, and their content, vary from time to time, but by browsing the web you will quickly find some options to choose between. In most cases, the tours consist of very small groups of tourists, who together explore the area. That is to say, no full busloads of people who, with cameras in hand, act like they are visiting a human zoo.

In the outskirts of the slums of Khlong Toey, very close to the tourist area of Sukhumvit, lies Khlong Toey Market, and it is quite easy to get here by yourself. It is located next to the intersection of Rama 3 Road and Rama 4 Road, just a couple of hundred meters off Sukhumvit soi 22 and 24. It is a massive market completely devoid of tourist attractions. And because of that, a place well worthy of a visit. The market is open more or less all day and all night, with the exception of four hours between 02.00 and 06.00. It can, however, be a bit dangerous to walk around by yourself in the area after midnight – on the other hand, as long as you are sober, and act with common sense, you are statistically safe almost everywhere in Bangkok.

Asia Revealed Publishing Company

<u>Inner-City Bike Rides</u>

Bangkok being a massive city, it is not always that easy to press through the tourist façade and get into the real spirit of the capital. Mainly because of the language barrier; a fact that can become really hard to handle when moving around off the beaten track. However, a good way of getting to see and experience real Thai neighborhoods is by bicycle accompanied by English speaking tour guides. Due to the heat, most bicycle tours of the city are arranged in the evening or at night. There are numerous organizers online, as well as many tours to sign up for once in Bangkok. They all, nevertheless, make sure that you get the chance to experience the *real* Bangkok. That is, the Bangkok of everyday people.

For those who cannot see themselves pedaling around on a bicycle in the at times oppressive humidity of Bangkok, there are some organizers who arrange these kinds of trips on Segways instead.

<u>Museum of Death: Siriraj Medical Museum</u>

On the west side of the river Chao Phraya, in the district of Bangkok Noi, lies the very esteemed state hospital Siriraj Hospital, which is the hospital most members of the Royal Family visit when in need. To get here, you need to cross the river, which can be done at a number of locations near the hospital. The closest pier is called Wang Lang, and the hospital is just a stone's throw away from it. The walk from Wang Lang is, in addition, really entertaining, since you will find a large market squeezed in between the narrow alleyways of the pier and the premises of the hospital. Alternatively, you can flag down a taxi anywhere in the city as all drivers know the location of Siriraj.

The hospital itself is very large and among the many buildings lies the odd and terrifying attraction of Siriraj Medical Museum. But do not be fooled – this is not about any dry lectures on the history of medical advancements, or boring displays and expositions stacked full of statistics and charts, but rather about the human body with all its faults and flaws. The museum is divided into five smaller museums, and in these sections the makeup of man is displayed in a way that does not shy away from anything. One section, for example, is dedicated to diseases, injuries, deformities, and genetic absurdities. However, the bodies and organs on display are no reproductions, but real. In the most macabre section of the museum, the Forensic Room, deceased people have been preserved by being lowered into giant containers of formaldehyde. The most notorious body of them all belongs to a serial killer that terrorized Bangkok during the 1950s.

This museum is not a carnival attraction, even though it might sound like it, but rather a serious exhibition in a nationally ground-breaking hospital. It is, though, utterly boundless, in all respects, and nothing is considered to be too offensive to show. A visit to the Museum of Death demands a strong stomach. Nevertheless, for anyone who is looking for a tourist attraction beyond the usual run-of-the-mill experience, or has a profound interest in the human body and what it looks like when being portrayed as anything but beautiful, a visit to the Museum of Death might come out as the most memorable moment of your Bangkok visit.

Wang Saen Suk Hell Garden

Among most everyday western people, the view of Buddhism has become somewhat warped, often due to the influence of various schools of Mindfulness. For example, you often hear people saying that Buddhism is more of a philosophy than a religion since there is no God to worship. Statements like these should, however, be taken with a grain of salt, since it is possible to be reborn as a god in Buddhism, in addition to the fact that Buddha himself has the status of God in many Buddhist traditions. Nonetheless, because of this perceived absence of a God – at least in the Christian, or perhaps Muslim, sense of the word – many westerners are also under the impression that there neither is a heaven nor a hell in Buddhism. This, no matter from what angle the issue is viewed, is far from the truth, which a visit to Wang Saen Suk Hell Garden will thoroughly prove.

Wang Saen Suk Hell Garden has been erected at a temple in the southeast of Bangkok to illustrate what is going on in Naraka, the Buddhist version of hell. At the entrance, you are greeted by a huge sign saying, "*Welcome to Hell*", which takes you to a large collection of macabre and violent displays with dolls and puppets ranging from life-size to veritable giants. The dolls are illustrating all the various punishments that you receive for different sins, and mixed in with the bloody puppets you will see, among other things, people being torn in half by hell-hounds, boiled alive in enormous cauldrons, and crushed to death in giant vices.

Whoever used to believe that Buddhism only was about karma and reincarnation in the form of earthly existences will be forced to severely adjust his or her point of view, since the Buddhist version of hell seems to be a lot nastier and more violent than most others. There are numerous so-called Gardens of Hell in Thailand, but this one is without a doubt one of the biggest. As with the Museum of Death at Siriraj Hospital, a trip to Wang Saen Suk Hell Garden is nothing for the faint-hearted, and young children should by no means experience it!

The easiest way to get to Wang Saen Suk Hell Garden is by taxi. The park lies in the neighboring town of Chonburi, which can be reached both day and night by fast buses from Ekkamai, the eastbound bus terminal of Bangkok. In addition, Chonburi is located by the sea, and if leaving Bangkok early in the morning, you will be able to exchange the oppressive heat of the inner city for beach walks, swimming, sunbathing and, of course, a stroll through Buddhist hell.

Thai Boxing – Muay Thai

Whether you are interested in sports or not, you should not miss the opportunity to go and see a Thai boxing fight, since the events entail so much more than just the bouts. Thai boxing, locally called Muay Thai, constitutes an integral part of Thai culture, and reflects many important cultural traits that can be found in the predominantly Buddhist society of Thailand. For example, the dance *"Wai Khruu"*, which is performed by the boxers before the fight starts.

Wai Khruu means "greet the teacher", and the gesture displays the profound respect that exists between laymen and various forms of superiors and seniors in Thailand, permeating every layer of all social orders, such as the relationship between novices and monks, between students and university lecturers, between employers and employees, between villagers and village headmen, between young and old, and between the Thai people and the Royal Family. Or, as in this case, between a fighter and his coach.

Visiting a Thai boxing stadium can be really intense, and if the main fight is between champions, a proper spectacle. It should be noted, though, that it can get pretty bloody, although fighters are rarely injured for life. In Bangkok, there are two Muay Thai stadiums. The oldest one is called Lumpini Boxing Stadium. The name comes from its former location at Lumpini Park. It has since then moved, and is now located near Don Muang Airport. If going here by yourself, the quickest way is to first cross town by skytrain, getting off at the end station Mor Chit on the Sukhumvit Line, and from there continue in a taxi. A far more convenient alternative, though, is to book a trip with a local travel agency, which will include transfer to and from any hotel in Bangkok. The other major boxing stadium is Rajadamner Stadium, which lies much closer to central Bangkok, more accurately between Khaosan Road and Dusit Zoo. A ticket costs between 500 and 2 000 baht, depending on how close to ringside you would like to sit, and if in need of transfer.

If you would like to train Muay Thai yourself during a visit, there are many good clubs in Bangkok with English speaking instructors. By a couple of searches on the

Internet, you will quickly find a gym suitable for the temporary visitor. The most fun alternative, though, might be the little gym tucked away at the end of Soi Rambutrii, just a stone's throw from Khaosan Road. At this place, you can pop in at any time during the day and pay for a Muay Thai lesson with a professional trainer. And once done, the madness of backpacker Khaosan is just around the corner, where you can relax your aching muscles with cold drinks and good music.

Asia Revealed Publishing Company

Travel Tips

Thailand is, in many respects, very different from most western countries, which you might not realize, or even think about, when lying there on the beach in Phuket or by the pool at a four or five-star hotel in Bangkok. Since you are almost always met with kindness and smiles by extremely accommodating drivers and waitresses, as well as all sorts of other staff members, it is all too easy to forget that there exist completely different sets of rules governing the social interaction between people in Thailand compared to England or perhaps the USA. To go through them all in these following paragraphs would, of course, be impossible. On the other hand, there are a couple of guidelines that everyone visiting Thailand should stick to in order to show respect, as well as to gain respect.

The most important rule concerns physical contact. In Thailand, there is a long tradition of placing what is holy high up in the air, and what is sinful next to the ground; a train of thought that is closely mirrored by how the Thais view the human body. You should, for example, never touch a person's head, while your feet must always be kept away. For example: to lovingly ruffle someone's hair is truly insulting. The only occasion when it is okay to touch someone's head is in the interaction between a parent and a child, or in the intimacy of the bedroom. In addition, when squatted on a mat having a traditional meal with someone from Thailand, bear in mind how, and where, you put your feet. And do not ever point with your feet at something or someone. To nonchalantly put your feet on a chair or, even worse, a table, is also extremely rude and inappropriate.

A second important feature of Thai society is the fact that Thais in general avoid conflicts. Thailand, as many other countries around Asia and the Middle East, is basically an honor culture, and people do their best to not lose face in public. One way of losing face is to be losing an argument, meaning that arguments, especially in public, should be handled like a normal conversation and with a somewhat apologetic attitude. Otherwise, there is a risk of things spiraling completely out of hand, resulting in people feeling the need to somehow retaliate to regain lost face.

Character traits that are deeply appreciated in Thailand, since they facilitate less conflicts and face-losing situations, are politeness, attentiveness, and self-control. By not screaming or acting in a threatening manner, you will be greeted by some of the nicest people in the world.

Traveling outside Bangkok

If you, for some reason, get tired of Bangkok and decide to head out into the rest of the country, then there are three major means of transportation to choose between: coach, train, or airplane.

The coaches depart from three different stations in Bangkok depending on the direction you are heading in. For trips to the north, you depart from Mor Chit Bus Terminal, which is located close to the skytrain station Mor Chit on the Sukhumvit Line. If going down south, or west towards the border to Burma, you need to take a taxi to the Southern Bus Terminal, which is located in a suburb west of the Chao Phraya river. And if you are heading eastwards, then you have to go to Ekkamai Bus Terminal, which is close to central Bangkok, just outside Ekkamai skytrain station on the Sukhumvit Line.

From these three bus terminals, coaches depart twenty-four hours a day to more or less all other towns and cities around Thailand. Usually you do not need to book any tickets in advance, just get on the first available one. And if traveling to other major cities in the country, you hardly ever have to wait for very long. You should, however, pay attention to what kind of coach you will end up on. There are both air-conditioned and non-air-conditioned coaches crossing Thailand, and although a non-air-conditioned one might be really cheap, it can also be brutally hot and uncomfortable.

The trains, on the other hand, depart from the central station Hua Lamphong, which lies right next to the subway station Hua Lamphong. Train tickets are sold in all sorts of varying classes, from air-conditioned private coupés to hard wooden chairs in cramped carriages. It is perfectly alright to buy a ticket on the spot; however, since they depart less frequently than the buses, it might be a good idea to book in advance.

The most convenient and fast way of traveling in Thailand, though, is by plane. And it is not uncommon that the plane tickets come cheaper than both the train tickets and the coach tickets. Two major budget airlines, Air Asia and Nok Air, have flights departing all day long to most big cities and towns in Thailand, usually from the old international airport of Don Muang, close to central Bangkok.

Other fast ways of getting around include picking up tickets on chartered VIP coaches or speedy minivans at hotels and tourist spots like Khaosan Road.

Asia Revealed Publishing Company

Good to Know

Sometimes bad things happen, and all of sudden you are lying there with a broken leg from a traffic accident. Or, perhaps, you have lost your passport, got your credit cards stolen, ended up in trouble with the local police, or contracted dengue fever.

In the following sections, you will find important information that could be very helpful in the face of troublesome situations.

Hospitals, Clinics, and Dentists

In Bangkok, you are never far from a hospital or a clinic. The hospitals in Bangkok are either privately run or state run. If you have a valid travel insurance, you are recommended to visit a private hospital, since they have long experience of dealing with tourists. These private hospitals range from small and efficient clinics to grand institutions resembling five-star hotels. Nevertheless, they all offer fairly identical treatments and care regarding most injuries and illnesses.

The state hospitals are recommended for people who, for one reason or another, have travelled to Thailand without a valid travel insurance. The price difference between a state hospital and a private hospital is astronomical – on the other hand, staying at a state hospital might not feel especially reassuring if dealing with complicated medical issues. Nonetheless, when it comes to fractured bones from traffic accidents, bouts of malaria and dengue fever, or any other common disease or injury that the Thai staff has long experience of treating, then the only worrying element of a visit to a state hospital are the at times really long ques.

For minor illnesses, which nevertheless must be medicated, for example, bad cases of tourist diarrhea, a visit to any of the myriad of clinics in Bangkok will suffice. Many of them accept travel insurances, however, since the cost of a visit often is less than the excess you sometimes must pay on your insurance policy, it might not be worth using it. If you need to visit a dentist, then you will not have to go far to find a private clinic. They are everywhere in Bangkok. The cost is low and for common, everyday procedures there is nothing to worry about regarding competence or skills. However, if a major surgical procedure is needed, you are advised to visit a private hospital, since most of them have their own practicing dentists.

Travel Insurance

When visiting Thailand, you should have some form of travel insurance. A travel insurance does not have to cost much, and in many cases, it might be part of the benefit package of your home insurance or bank account. Nevertheless, it is definitely worth spending a bit on a travel insurance since being hospitalized in Thailand for a longer period of time can generate bills in the millions of baht.

Traffic

The traffic situation in Thailand is truly disheartening, with an unrivalled number of casualties. During the last couple of years, Thailand has on and off secured the position of the deadliest country in the entire world, out beating much poorer and less developed nations in South America and Africa. If something would happen while visiting Thailand, it most likely will be traffic related.

There are, on the other hand, a handful of precautionary measures that can be taken to reduce the risk considerably. First and foremost; go by taxi instead of tuk-tuk since most taxis will have seat belts (however, do not bet on it!); book taxis in advance when traveling long distances as they can provide car safety seats for children; do not ride motorcycles or scooters on heavily trafficked roads; remember that you cannot trust the street lights as many drivers have the bad habit of increasing their speed instead of slowing down when the lights switch; and if traveling across the country, opt for train or plane instead of coach. In addition, there will always be footbridges available in either direction when crossing major streets in Bangkok.

Diseases and Dangerous Animals

Thailand is a tropical country and the home of roughly 10% of all the species of the world, meaning that there are more creatures to be aware of, and which you should do your best to avoid. The animals causing the most damage, suffering, and deaths are not the big ones, but the small ones: spiders, scorpions, snakes, jellyfish, centipedes, and, of course, mosquitoes and parasites.

With the exception of parasites present in spoiled food and bad water, in Bangkok there is not that much to worry about. In most neighborhoods, the councils have been very effective in keeping the mosquito population down, and you hardly ever get bitten.

In the countryside and on the islands, however, the situation is completely different. Here you need to be aware that it is essential to avoid getting bitten by mosquitos. It is also in the country and, of course, on the islands that you will encounter most spiders, snakes, and jellyfish, among other dangerous creatures. The most lethal ones are the jellyfish, since both spiders and snakes do their best to avoid humans. Nonetheless, there are several snake species in Thailand that carry enough poison to kill within hours. So, if being bit, no matter what the snake looks like, get to a hospital as fast as possible. And when swimming in the sea, it is recommended to beforehand ask around if any jellyfish has been spotted – the matter of fact is that several species of jellyfish float past the coastline of Thailand regularly and some of them, such as the box jellyfish, can be deadly.

Apart from various stomach illnesses, dengue fever is one of the most common tropical diseases in the country. Dengue fever manifests itself, most often, as a severe flu with high fever and aching muscles. There is no cure; nevertheless, you should be under surveillance of trained nurses since there is a risk of deadly complications. For a generally healthy person, it is possible to attract dengue fever without even realizing it, since it might only show itself as a light flu. Nevertheless, if having a fever for more than three days, always contact a doctor.

Power Sockets and Electrical Wires

All sorts of electrical wirings and installations in Thailand are of a substandard quality. It is not uncommon, even in hotels with four or five stars, to see small electrical flames shooting out of power sockets when plugging in or unplugging a device.

To a certain degree, this problem is beyond one's control, which, on the other hand, does not mean that you should accept a dangerous situation. If the wiring is of a low quality, ask to change rooms. Or, in a worst-case scenario, check into another hotel. You should also be aware of low hanging power lines out on the streets and around swimming pools.

The Royal Thai Police

The police in Thailand, that you as a traveler may come in contact with, is divided into the regular force and the tourist force. If possible, always contact the tourist police first, since they have staff members that can speak English. You are recommended to write down their number when arriving at the international airport Suvarnabhumi.

The regular force, however, can be a bit tricky to deal with, especially if you have committed a crime. Most of the crimes committed by tourists in Thailand are traffic related, that is, people driving either drunk or without helmets. These situations can usually be handled quickly, sometimes even without being brought to the police station. However, if caught with drugs, no matter how small the amount is, you are in serious trouble. It is not unusual that life in prison is sentenced out to people carrying quantities that in many other countries would just amount to a short stint.

The laws governing the use of narcotics are not the only laws that are extremely strict. The laws concerning the Royal Family are even stricter, and you are strongly advised to never talk about anyone in the Royal Family in a derogatory manner. By insulting the Royal Institution, you are likely to face up to 25 years in jail.

Asia Revealed Publishing Company

Final Thoughts

After having read what I have written I realize that there are a number of other attractions and places that I should have mentioned. However, as pointed out in the introduction, it is impossible to go through every single little thing about a city as colorful, immense, and strange as Bangkok.

Something that is distinctive of Bangkok, though, is that one event always, and inevitably, leads to another. That is, it is hard to stick to an itinerary when exploring this sprawling city, because as soon as you leave your hotel you bump into other travelers and tourists offering suggestions about places to see and things to do.

Thus, the attractions and destinations mentioned in *Bangkok in a Nutshell* are not the only ones worthy of a visit. There are plenty of other fun, exciting and, not least, thought-provoking things to do. And the easiest way to find these, at times, hidden gems is to speak with the people you meet. This is particularly evident when visiting a place like Khaosan Road, where you most likely will run into travelers whose only plan was to get to this backpacker Mecca to see what would happen next. And that something *will* happen, is a given.

This, if anything, is Bangkok in a nutshell.